NEW TESTAMENT MESSAGE

A Biblical-Theological Commentary
Wilfrid Harrington, O.P. and Donald Senior, C.P.
EDITORS

New Testament Message, Volume 12

GALATIANS

Carolyn Osiek, R.S.C.J.

Michael Glazier, Inc.
Wilmington, Delaware

MICHAEL GLAZIER, INC.
1210A King Street
Wilmington, Delaware 19801

Library of Congress Catalog Card Number: 80-66456
International Standard Book Number
    New Testament Message series: 0-89453-123-9
    GALATIANS: 0-89453-135-2

Printed in the United States of America by Abbey Press

Contents

EDITORS' PREFACE

New Testament Message is a commentary series designed to bring the best of biblical scholarship to a wide audience. Anyone who is sensitive to the mood of the church today is aware of a deep craving for the Word of God. This interest in reading and praying the scriptures is not confined to a religious elite. The desire to strengthen one's faith and to mature in prayer has brought Christians of all types and all ages to discover the beauty of the biblical message. Our age has also been heir to an avalanche of biblical scholarship. Recent archaeological finds, new manuscript evidence, and the increasing volume of specialized studies on the Bible have made possible a much more profound penetration of the biblical message. But the flood of information and its technical nature keeps much of this scholarship out of the hands of the Christian who is eager to learn but is not a specialist. *New Testament Message* is a response to this need.

The subtitle of the series is significant: "A Biblical-Theological Commentary." Each volume in the series, while drawing on up-to-date scholarship, concentrates on bringing to the fore in understandable terms the specific message of each biblical author. The essay-format (rather than a word-by-word commentary) helps the reader savor the beauty and power of the biblical message and, at the same time, understand the sensitive task of responsible biblical interpretation.

A distinctive feature of the series is the amount of space given to the "neglected" New Testament writings, such as Colossians, James, Jude, the Pastoral Letters, the Letters of Peter and John. These briefer biblical books make a significant but often overlooked contribution to the richness of the New Testament. By assigning larger than normal coverage to these books, the series hopes to give these parts of Scripture the attention they deserve.

Because *New Testament Message* is aimed at the entire English speaking world, it is a collaborative effort of international proportions. The twenty-two contributors represent biblical scholarship in North America, Britain, Ireland and Australia. Each of the contributors is a recognized expert in his or her field, has published widely, and has been chosen because of a proven ability to communicate at a popular level. And, while all of the contributors are Roman Catholic, their work is addressed to the Christian community as a whole. The New Testament is the patrimony of all Christians.It is the hope of all concerned with this series that it will bring a fuller appreciation of God's saving Word to his people.

Wilfrid Harrington, O.P.
Donald Senior, C.P.

To Sharon, Arlene, and Martha
from whom I have learned much
about Christian freedom

INTRODUCTION

GALATIANS IS A LETTER that is concerned from start to finish with a question that is timely in any age: the freedom of the Christian. Paul was aware that this freedom must be fought for simultaneously on two fronts. It must be defended against laws and restrictions imposed from without. At the same time, freedom is equally threatened from within by the innate human tendency to abuse it as an excuse for selfishness.

The Letter to the Galatians consists of six chapters which can be rather neatly divided into three units. Chapters 1 and 2 give the background and set the stage for Paul's argument. Chapters 3 and 4 are concerned with the freedom from the Jewish Law upon which Paul insists. Chapters 5 and 6 deal with the character of true inner freedom.

Paul saw the rending that could occur in Christian communities of his day when some observed the prescriptions of the Jewish Law (circumcision, sabbath, food laws, etc.) and others did not. Common worship and table fellowship were severely impaired. With his keen sense of the unity of Christians in the Body of Christ, he saw this as an intolerable situation. Even more, the centrality of Christ was compromised by the belief that observance of the regulations of the Law had some part in the action of God whereby we are saved. If the Law is also necessary, Paul reasoned, then Christ is not the sole and unique way to salvation. But of course he is. This conviction led Paul into combat with those who advocated Christian adoption of practices of the Law.

That is what happened in Galatia. Paul was one of the first to preach the Gospel there. After his departure, however, another group of Christian missionaries came and suggested that Paul's message was not complete: observance of at least some of the tenets of the Mosaic Law was also necessary. Exactly who these Judaizing Christians were remains a mystery. We can only conjecture from Paul's own statements here and in his other letters, as well as some information from the Acts of the Apostles, that they were Jewish converts to Christianity who set out to harmonize their former faith with their new one much more extensively than Paul was willing to do. It has even been suggested, rather convincingly, that we have a short fragment of their argumentation in 2 Cor 6:14–7:1, a passage that has long been recognized by biblical scholars as a foreign intrusion into Paul's text (see the second entry for H.D. Betz in Suggestions for Further Reading at the end of this volume).

In response to this threat to his convictions about Christ and his Church, Paul wrote the Letter to the Galatians during the middle years of his missionary career, probably between 50 and 55 A.D., perhaps during his long stay in Ephesus (see 1 Cor 16:8; Acts 19:1-10), though nothing can be known for sure about date and place of writing. In the letter he returned to the assumptions underlying the Law in Judaism: the covenant and promise given to Abraham. By ingenious exegesis of a series of biblical texts and use of several aptly-chosen comparisons, Paul demonstrates in chapters 3 and 4 that the promise given to Abraham antedated the giving of the Law, and that observance of the Law is merely one response to God's initiative in the giving of the covenant. The Christian's response is to be different. It is the free and generous service of those who give themselves over to Christ and his loved ones through spontaneous response to the inspiration of the Spirit rather than obedience to the stipulations of the Law.

A few words of explanation should be given with regard to Paul's use of Scripture and exegetical method, especially prominent in chapter 3 of Galatians. His line of argument is very difficult to follow for the Western reader who expects clear, logical steps leading to a conclusion. Paul is using the texts in quite a different way, the time-honored way of the rabbis from whom he learned it. This rabbinic method of exegesis has most abundantly survived in the Talmud, the extensive collection of opinions of the early rabbis on questions of interpretation of the Law. Its starting point is the assumption that, since all Scripture is the inspired word of God, it is valid and true in all of its parts as well as in its entirety. Therefore any passage may retain its validity even in a new context where it is really applied to something very different than it was originally. We who have grown accustomed to the historical-critical method with its great attention to understanding a passage within its historical and social context may find Paul's method quite foreign. He is simply using the tools he learned and which were normally accepted in his world, just as we do in ours.

Because of his controversial attitude toward the Law, Paul has always been a source of contention between Christians and Jews. Even in the first centuries after his death Jews and Jewish Christians accused him of perverting the preaching of Jesus and totally misunderstanding the positive, life-giving aspect of the Mosaic Law, portraying it instead as a sinister force keeping its subjects in slavery. Recent scholarship has shown the variety of attitudes toward the Law within first-century Judaism itself and has suggested that Paul may not have been so far-out on this question as had been previously thought. Still the extremely oppressive picture of the Law which Paul paints has never been satisfactorily explained except in terms of an exaggerated reaction to competing preachers whose success as well as the implications of their teaching were a great threat to him.

Since the Protestant Reformation of the sixteenth century Paul has also been a source of contention between Catholics and Protestants. Luther, building on the insights of Augustine 1100 years earlier, found in Paul's principle of justification by faith in Christ rather than through the works of the

Law the fundamental insight he needed to set himself free from the heavily devotional Christianity of the Middle Ages and find assurance of personal salvation. Paul has been ever since the patron saint of Protestantism, while Catholicism has relied more on John's mystical union, Luke's extension of the Church into the world in history, and especially Matthew's attempt to lay the foundations for the New Law of the New People of God. Again, recent assessments on both sides have shown that Paul is more the proclaimer of the free gift of salvation in Christ than he is champion of the individual conscience.

Considering the sign of contradiction that Paul has frequently been in the history of Christianity, it is probably no accident that in the Letter to the Galatians there is a great paradox: this letter of Paul which speaks most eloquently about freedom is also the one in which the cross of Christ is most frequently mentioned. In Gal 2:20; 3:1; 5:24; and 6:12,14 Paul speaks of the mystery of Christ's suffering death as part of the mystery of his own life and death. Of all the New Testament writers, Paul is one who most creatively and most profoundly (as well as earliest) was able to take the instrument of Jesus' final humiliation and transform it into a powerful positive symbol in the life of the Christian. The life of the Christian, lived in conformity to that of Jesus, was to share in his suffering and death in order to share in his resurrection. The Letter to the Galatians is a major contribution to Paul's theology of the cross.

Unity with Christ in and through the community was one priority for Paul and he could therefore not tolerate dissension. Freedom from outer and inner restraints in order to be able to follow the lead of the Spirit was the other. These two, unity and freedom, are the two complementary foundations upon which Paul's pastoral theology rests. To see them as Paul saw them is to understand his contribution to Christian tradition. While the subject of unity is more fully explored in other letters, notably 1 Corinthians, that of freedom is the heart and soul of the Epistle to the Galatians.

I. GREETING AND INTRODUCTION 1:1-9

PAUL'S SELF-IDENTITY.
1:1.

> Paul an apostle—not from men nor through man, but through Jesus Christ and God the Father, who raised him from the dead—

Paul begins his letter to the Galatians, as he does all his letters, according to the common form of greeting used by letter writers of his day. The opening words are the name of the sender and his identification. Thus Paul is above all apostle to his congregations, and that is a favorite way of identifying himself (compare Rom 1:1; 1 Cor 1:1; 2 Cor 1:1). Elsewhere he will simply add "of Christ Jesus" (1 and 2 Cor).

Apostleship in the first Christian generation consisted of being sent by someone, usually a community, as a missionary to preach the gospel and as a delegate or ambassador from one community to another. Thus the apostolic role carried two distinct types of responsibility: to plant the Word in the hearts of those who had not yet heard it, and to nourish that Word by repeated contact and communication with believers.

Paul's purpose in writing the letter is to defend his own understanding of the gospel. Even though he was probably officially commissioned as apostle by the Church of Antioch (see Acts 13:2-3), and though he later shows that he is in communication with Jerusalem (Gal 1:18-19; 2:7-10), he is here quite explicit about the original source of his apostolic credentials: they came neither from nor through the mediation of human sources but through Jesus Christ himself (see vs. 12) and ultimately from God who vindicated Jesus in the resurrection.

LOCATION OF THE RECIPIENTS.
1:2.

> ²and all the brethren who are with me,
>   To the churches of Galatia:

Paul includes in a general way in his greeting others who are with him, but does not name them as he sometimes does in other letters (see 1 Cor 1:1; 2 Cor 1:1; Phil 1:1; 1 Thess 1:1; 2 Thess 1:1). The second element of the ancient letter greeting appears at the end of vs. 2: the identification of the recipients. It is clear therefore that this is a circular letter, intended to be sent around and read in a number of churches—how many we unfortunately do not know. Nor do we know what exactly Paul means by "Galatia." He may be referring to the geographical region comprising most of north central Asia Minor, in which we have almost no evidence that he preached (except perhaps Acts 16:6-7; 18:23). The more likely possibility is that he means the Roman province of Galatia, which also contained territory further south, southeast, and southwest, including cities in Pisidia and Lycaonia in which Acts records missionary visits by Paul: Antioch of Pisidia, Iconium, Lystra and Derbe (Acts 13:14–14:23; 16:1-5). In either case we know from the rest of the letter that the communities to whom Paul writes are ones in which he and his companions were the first to preach the gospel.

BLESSING.
1:3-5.

> [3]Grace to you and peace from God the Father and our Lord Jesus Christ, [4]who gave himself for our sins to deliver us from the present evil age, according to the will of our God and Father; [5]to whom be the glory for ever and ever. Amen.

The third element in the greeting of the ancient letter is contained in these verses: a wish for the welfare of the recipients. This salutation is transformed by Paul into a blessing and credal statement, a brief, pithy formulation of belief in the redemptive role of Jesus and the necessary stance of the Christian who awaits immediate deliverance from this present life. The wording is probably borrowed from a formula of community prayer. It ends with the liturgical affirmation "amen," or "so be it," that was adopted by Christians from Jewish liturgical prayer and preserved in the original Hebrew (compare 1 Chr 16:36; Neh 5:13; 1 Cor 14:16).

Comparison of the opening lines of Paul's letters with other examples of letters written by his contemporaries reveals the similarity of structure. A personal letter, for example, might begin: "Aristarchos to his sister Eutyche, greeting. I pray that you are well and the gods have smiled upon you."

The prayer for the recipients and even the blessing are notably short and succinct here in comparison to most Pauline letters (see for example 1 Cor 1:3-9; Phil 1:2-11). The impression cannot be avoided that Paul is so disturbed by what he has heard of the events in Galatia and therefore by what he will have to say that he is not in the mood for pleasantries, but wants to get on with the matter at hand.

OCCASION OF THE LETTER.
1:6-9.

> [6]I am astonished that you are so quickly deserting him who called you in the grace of Christ and turning to a different gospel—[7]not that there is another gospel, but there are some who trouble you and want to pervert the gospel of Christ. [8]But even if we, or an angel from heaven, should preach to you a gospel contrary to that which we preached to you, let him be accursed. [9]As we have said before, so now I say again, If any one is preaching to you a gospel contrary to that which you received, let him be accursed.

These verses make it fairly clear what has happened in Galatia, at least as Paul sees it. He has preached the gospel of Jesus Christ there as he understands and believes it. It is the proclamation of the crucified and risen Christ who died to redeem us from our sins and was raised on the third day, all in keeping with the prophecy of the Scriptures (1 Cor 15:3-4). Christ is the one who is the total fulfillment of all the promises of God (2 Cor 1:20), even though his way through humiliation and suffering to glory is a stumbling block that seems like utter stupidity to those who do not understand (1 Cor 1:20-25).

Now Paul feels that the Galatians have deserted him and the truth by turning to "a different gospel." He hastens to add that there can be only one gospel, but that it can be twisted and perverted, and this is just what has happened. He calls down upon those who would lead them astray the formal curse that is the exact opposite of the wish for grace and peace expressed above (vs. 3). He seeks to include every possibility of error and to sweep it away, hence the hypothetical example in vs. 8 by which even he or an angel from heaven is not to escape falling under the curse. There are to be no exceptions.

"As we have said before" at the beginning of vs. 9 most likely refers to more than just the preceding verse. Paul has undoubtedly warned them before of such dangers in much the same language. However, the repetition of the condemnation in vss. 8 and 9 creates a sense of great solemnity.

We shall have occasion later to examine who these people are who are preaching the gospel differently, and what is their way of preaching it (see comment on Gal 2:3-5; 5:1-12). It may be helpful to note here that the threat of divergent teaching is not confined to Galatia. Many letters written by Paul and others in his wake are concerned with the refuting of different approaches to the mystery of Christ. The "super apostles" of 2 Corinthians 11:5 and 12:11 apparently preached at Corinth a gospel of eloquence and wisdom, signs and wonders. Some at Thessalonica were over-eager for the final coming of Christ and settled into a lazy and irresponsible way of life as a result (2 Thess 2:1-3; 3:10-12), inciting people by rumor and perhaps even forged letters (2:2). The Pastoral Epistles condemn those who advocate abstinence in matters of marriage and food (1 Tim 4:3) and who say that the resurrection is already completed rather than to come (2 Tim 2:18). Divergent teachers in Philippi seem to be talking quite similarly to those in Galatia, saying that the Mosaic Law must still be observed, at least in some of its external regulations (Phil 3:2-3).

II. AUTOBIOGRAPHICAL DEFENSE 1:10 – 2:14

THE SOURCE OF PAUL'S AUTHORITY.
1:10-12.

> [10]Am I now seeking the favor of men, or of God? Or am I trying to please men? If I were still pleasing men, I should not be a servant of Christ.
>
> [11]For I would have you know, brethren, that the gospel which was preached by me is not man's gospel [12]For I did not receive it from man, nor was I taught it, but it came through a revelation of Jesus Christ.

At this point Paul begins a long personal defense of his ministry and of his right to preach the gospel as he preaches it. His commission, he claims, is not based on human authority (see 1:1). At the heart of his experience of having been selected, called, and sent forth is the assurance that it is God who so impels him. It was through a first-hand encounter with the risen Christ that Paul received his apostolic credentials (vs. 12).

These words are undoubtedly a reference to his "conversion" experience, however it may have happened. The three accounts in Acts (9:1-9; 22:6-11; 26:12-18) are each slightly different in detail. They portray it as a spectacular occurrence on the road to Damascus with many of the characteristics of divine manifestations that are used by other writers of Paul's day: dazzling light that knocks the recipient to the ground and a heavenly voice to identify the revealer and give instructions (compare Matt 17:2-7 and parallels; John 18:4-6; Rev 1:13-20). Paul himself is much more reticent in describing what happened. From him we have only Gal 1:12, 15-16; Phil 3:7-11; 1 Cor 15:8-10; and perhaps 2 Cor 12:1-10. Whatever the way in which Christ broke through to him, it is quite clear that the inward effect worked in Paul was both personally wrenching and disorienting (Phil 3:7-11), and at the same time was translated very quickly into apostolic outpouring (Gal 1:15-17).

With Paul's keen sense of commissioning and dedication to the gospel, it would be totally impossible that he should still be looking for human approval, or that his motives should be self-seeking in raising the objections he is about to pose in the letter that follows (vs. 10).

What literary models is Paul following? In vs. 10 we have the first example in Galatians of a literary style common to Greek writers of the period, one which is a favorite of Paul. It is called by scholars the "Stoic-Cynic diatribe" because it was largely developed by writers of those philosophical schools during the Hellenistic age, that period of rapid expansion of Greek culture throughout the eastern Mediterranean following the conquest of the whole area by the armies of the Macedonian, Alexander the Great, in the third century B.C. The diatribe form is recognizable by the short, blunt, testy statements and questions posed to an imaginary listener; sometimes the questions are abruptly answered before the author proceeds (for examples, see: Gal 3:1-5; 1 Cor 1:20; 3:5; 9:1-8; Rom 3:1, 27-31; Jas 2:5-7; 4:13-5:6).

In vss. 11-12 Paul reiterates and elaborates the point he has established in the opening lines of the letter: his primary authorization for preaching the Gospel the way he does does not stem from any human delegation. Rather, the command to apostleship was given to him directly from Jesus Christ — by revelation! The sheer audacity of the claim is stupendous. Probably never having known the historical Jesus, Paul can still see himself as directly entrusted with his commission by the risen Jesus Christ himself. Such confidence in one's spiritual experience is awesome. Even though Paul did eventually "check it out" (see Gal 2:2), he still maintains that the role of human intermediaries was minimal.

Here again the consideration of literary models is important, and can give us some clues how to understand Paul. Beginning with these verses and continuing into the whole section that follows through most of chapter 2, he is most likely following the literary convention of the formal "apology," a form that would have been familiar to him from his Greek literary education. It consists in a lively, colorful explanation of one's conduct, delivered in such a way as to extraordinarily impress the hearers or readers and persuade them of one's sincerity, rationality, innocence of a charge, or whatever the speaker or writer has at stake. It is meant to be an exposition of what the writer is all about, what "makes him tick," and would have been known to Paul especially from the Greek philosophers, beginning with Socrates as depicted by Plato. It is not hard to imagine how, in the attempt to stress certain important points, the other side of the story may be neglected. It is of the very nature of persuasion that I cannot give equal time to both sides. Thus while this autobiographical section of Galatians is of immense importance in providing details about Paul's life and attitudes, we must remember that he is being highly subjective, and that a certain amount of bias may also be present.

PAUL THE JEW.
1:13-14.

> [13]For you have heard of my former life in Judaism, how I persecuted the church of God violently and tried to destroy it; [14]and I advanced in Judaism beyond many of my own age among my people, so extremely zealous was I for the traditions of my fathers.

Paul presumes that the Galatian Christians know his background and that he need only summarize it here. They probably heard it from Paul himself. He is not ashamed of his past, for at the time it seemed good (vs. 14 and Phil 3:4-6). He was an ardent young Pharisee, a member of that group who represented the most progressive scholars of the Law in his day. His ardor led him to be an outstanding leader, one of the most promising figures in the upcoming generation. His enthusiasm for the purity and quality of religious observance led him even to offer to seek out and track down those who would compromise the faith and traditions of his ancestors by daring to introduce innovations that were not acceptable to those on whose sound teaching he relied—the great rabbis of Jerusalem (see Acts 22:3).

It was in this capacity, with full delegation from the Jerusalem authorities, that Paul began to pursue those who claimed that the Messiah was Jesus of Nazareth who had been crucified by the Romans. Paul was an official agent of the Jewish authorities sent to arrest and even to treat "violently" (vs. 13) these followers of the Nazarene (see too 1 Cor 15:9; Acts 9:1-2; 22:4-5; 26:9-11).

"CONVERSION" AND RESULTS.
1:15-17.

> [15]But when he who had set me apart before I was born, and had called me through his grace, [16]was pleased to reveal his Son to me, in order that I might preach him among the Gentiles, I did not confer with flesh and blood, [17]nor did I go up to Jerusalem to those who were apostles before me, but I went away into Arabia; and again I returned to Damascus.

In spite of the dramatic way in which the Acts of the Apostles portrays what we have come to call Paul's "conversion," Paul himself always refers to it very simply (see also Phil 3:7-11). We hear in vs. 15 echoes of the prophetic calling from Jeremiah (1:5) and Second Isaiah (49:1). Paul alludes to texts that are a familiar part of his theological background, but he is also consciously placing himself in line with the "greats" of his religious tradition.

"Conversion" is probably not the best way to call what happened to Paul, though it has come to be the acceptable name for his experience. Popular usage suggests only two ways to see a conversion: from bad to good and from one religion or denomination to another. Actually what happened to Paul was neither. He certainly was not moving from sin to grace, for he tells us quite clearly in Phil 3:6 that he was a blameless observer of the Law, which is the way to holiness and knowledge of God for the believing Jew. Nor was his a change from one religion to another. Christians at that point in history, only a few years after the death of Jesus, were still seen as members of the Jewish community, whether by birth or, for Gentiles, by formal entry into that community as proselytes, though many of the believers in Jesus may also have been Gentiles more loosely associated with the Synagogue (perhaps the "God-fearers" of texts like Acts 16:14 and 18:7). They were a not-easily-definable group within Judaism with a very different point of view about what the scriptures and the prophecies meant. By this time they were meeting together privately in homes to share the common meal and reflect together on the scriptures, but they still worshiped in the Temple in Jerusalem (Acts 2:46) and probably joined in Synagogue worship in other areas as long as they were still welcome.

Paul's experience can properly be called a conversion only in the deeper sense of a psychic or spiritual conversion. It was a startling change of perspective which required tearing down the whole value system he had previously built up and constructing a new set of values and social patterns based on his new conviction that Jesus of Nazareth is indeed Christ and Lord. The radicalness of his change was not unlike that of a prominent figure in one of the major Christian Churches who suddenly abandons his former position and joins a small, "far-out," and very suspect sect.

What is striking about the change that took place in Paul, at least as he describes it in retrospect twenty years later, is that it is not at all an introspective experience, but rather one which impels him outwards. He is a man with a mission. He states that he did not, as might have been expected, go at once to pay his respect to the leaders of the Jerusalem Church. He might not have been believed or accepted if he had tried. "Arabia" to which he retreated instead probably means the area just west and south of Judea, the kingdom of the Nabataeans with their capital at Petra in what is today southern Jordan. There may already have been small groups of Christians living in the midst of these people who prospered because of their location along the trade route to the East. His departure from Damascus at the end of a visit there seems not to have been very pleasant (see 2 Cor 11:32-33; Acts 9:23).

TRIP TO JERUSALEM.
1:18-20.

> [18]Then after three years I went up to Jerusalem to visit Cephas, and remained with him fifteen days. [19]But I saw none of the other apostles except James the Lord's brother. [20](In what I am writing to you, before God, I do not lie!)

Finally Paul returned to Jerusalem for his first visit as a Christian. His aim was not to visit widely, but to confer with the community leaders. He spent most of his time with Cephas. Paul uses interchangeably this Aramaic version and the Greek version of Peter's name (compare 2:7-9). For two weeks he talked with Peter, probably listened to his preaching, and learned the traditions of this group who comprised most of those who had known Jesus.

The only other person in Jerusalem who is mentioned by name is James, the Lord's brother. He was not one of the twelve, but was a near relative of Jesus and a revered figure in the early church, one of those to whom a key appearance of the risen Jesus was attributed (1 Cor 15:7).

He held a position of prominence with Peter and John in the Jerusalem community (Acts 12:17; 15:13) and seems to have remained in leadership there when they were no longer present (Acts 21:18). Later legends attribute to him the authorship of writings about the childhood of Jesus, and a reliable tradition tells of his death at the instigation of the Sanhedrin a few years before the uprising of 66-70 A.D.

Paul's point here is what has already been strongly stated in vss. 11-12 and 16-17: his authority does not depend mainly on any human delegation, in spite of apparent accusations to the contrary.

MISSIONARY ACTIVITY.
1:21-24.

> [21]Then I went into the regions of Syria and Cilicia. [22]And I was still not known by sight to the churches of Christ in Judea; [23]they only heard it said, "He who once persecuted us is now preaching the faith he once tried to destroy." [24]And they glorified God because of me.

After his first visit to Jerusalem Paul set out in missionary work. First he probably became affiliated with the church of Antioch in Syria, and perhaps spent some time there getting to know the community and learning about the rapidly developing Christian tradition in an environment that was more influenced by Greek customs and ways of thinking than the Jerusalem group would have been.

The Antioch of Paul's day was the third greatest city of the Empire after Rome and Alexandria, a thriving metropolis of racial and cultural mixture in which Greek was the official language though large segments of the population spoke Syriac, a Semitic language closely related to Aramaic and Hebrew. Historical and archeological sources indicate a large and influential Jewish population in the city. Acts 11:19 describes the formation of the first group of Christians during the disarray following the murder of Stephen in Jerusalem. It was apparently at Antioch that the first conscious effort was made to evangelize Gentiles (Acts

11:21), and there that the group received for the first time its Greek name, "Christians," followers of the Christ. This use of the Greek equivalent of the title Messiah as part of the proper name of Jesus quickly became regular usage even among Gentiles for whom the title Messiah must have had very little meaning (see vs. 22).

From Antioch Paul set forth with Barnabas as an officially delegated missionary (Acts 13:1-3). The trip to Cyprus and south-central Asia Minor referred to here by Paul is probably that described in Acts, chapters 13 and 14. In the meantime, the news of his changed status and success as a missionary spread as far as Judea and was a source of joy and amazement.

MEETING IN JERUSALEM.
2:1-2.

> **2** Then after fourteen years I went up again to Jerusalem with Barnabas, taking Titus along with me. ²I went up by revelation; and I laid before them (but privately before those who were of repute) the gospel which I preach among the Gentiles, lest somehow I should be running or had run in vain.

The fourteen years that elapsed between Paul's first and second visits to Jerusalem need not all have been spent "on the road" in missionary activity. As has been said above, some of that time at the beginning was undoubtedly spent settling in at Antioch. Upon their return from the field, Paul and Barnabas would also have spent some time in "R and R," enjoying their homecoming and reporting on the success of their venture (see Acts 14:26-28). It is not difficult to imagine the mixed joy and curiosity with which these laborers in the far-flung field were received by those who had sent them out. In spite of frequent communication by letter during the time away, their first-hand account would be worth far more.

After some time at Antioch, Paul returned to Jerusalem with Barnabas and Titus, another co-worker, a Gentile.

While Paul emphasizes the unusual cause of the trip (by
revelation), Acts 15:2 says rather prosaically that they were
delegated by the community. The two accounts need not be
contradictory: when Paul simply says in Gal 1:21 that he
went to Cilicia, Acts 13:2-3 indicates that this missionary
journey was inspired by prophetic revelation.

The purpose of the trip was discussion of an issue that
was quite central to Paul's theology and to the message
of Galatians. There was disagreement between some in the
Jerusalem Church and others, especially at Antioch, over
whether Gentile converts, whose numbers were growing,
should be made to observe the whole Mosaic Law just as
if they were pious Jews. Paul's instinct to check things out
with the original group of leaders again shows itself. He
wishes to discuss privately with the Jerusalem leaders (Peter,
James and John), but in the presence of his two witnesses,
Barnabas and Titus, what he sees as the new but valid
direction in which the Antioch-based Church is moving.
He believes that the clear success of the Gentile mission in
which he has been engaged proves that the hand of God is
behind this venture.

CONFLICT OVER TITUS.
2:3-5.

> [3]But even Titus, who was with me, was not compelled to
> be circumcised, though he was a Greek. [4]But because of
> false brethren secretly brought in, who slipped in to spy
> out our freedom which we have in Christ Jesus, that they
> might bring us into bondage—[5]to them we did not yield
> submission even for a moment, that the truth of the gospel
> might be preserved for you.

The issue at stake in this second Jerusalem visit is observance of the Mosaic Law on the part of Gentile converts.
In order to support his contention that his position was
recognized and sanctioned by the Jerusalem authorities,
Paul here points out that one of his companions to the
meeting was not even Jewish. Titus was a Gentile, and there

was no official pressure to force him into observing the Law, which would be symbolized by acceptance of circumcision.

Though there was no pressure from the community leaders, there certainly was a problem originating somewhere else. The "false brethren secretly brought in" are not readily identifiable. They seem, however, to have come from the opposing party, that is, the element in the Jerusalem Church that was insisting on circumcision and full legal observance (sabbath, food laws, etc.) on the part of anyone who wanted to join the community. Paul, on the contrary, was convinced that the "freedom which we have in Christ Jesus" removed all necessity of legal observance. He appears here the same as he appears throughout his missionary career: unswerving on this point.

It would seem from the way he expresses himself in this passage and elsewhere (for example 2:14,19) that his conviction about freedom from the Law extended not only to Gentile converts but to himself and other Jewish Christians as well. For those who are in the freedom brought by Christ, whether Gentile or Jew, there is no longer any need for the Law.

RECOGNITION OF THE GENTILE MISSION. 2:6-9.

> [6]And from those who were reputed to be something (what they were makes no difference to me; God shows no partiality)—those, I say, who were of repute added nothing to me; [7]but on the contrary, when they saw that I had been entrusted with the gospel to the uncircumcised, just as Peter had been entrusted with the gospel to the circumcised [8](for he who worked through Peter for the mission to the circumcised worked through me also for the Gentiles), [9]and when they perceived the grace that was given to me, James and Cephas and John, who were reputed to be pillars, gave to me and Barnabas the right hand of fellowship, that we should go to the Gentiles and they to the circumcised;

Again Paul asserts his basic independence from the Jerusalem Church (see above, 1:12, 16, 19) and again we must realize the apologetic or defensive nature of the letter. It is to the advantage of the argument he is constructing to show that his position is essentially rooted in divine authorization which is then approved from Jerusalem.

There is a slight edge of cynicism in Paul's language in vs. 6, perhaps reflecting his exasperation at the inconsistency of Cephas which he will discuss later at 2:11-14. Those who are given recognition by others—namely, the Jerusalem leaders—are really nothing more than God makes of them, and God of course is impartial. The idea of the impartiality of God and therefore of those who would be his faithful servants is an important one in Jewish theology (see Lev 19:15; Dt 10:17; Sir 35:12-13; Jas 2:1-9).

Vss. 7-9 describe the understanding reached by Paul and Barnabas with James, Cephas (Peter), and John, the three recognized Jerusalem leaders. Those in Jerusalem acknowledged that the obvious success of the Gentile mission in Syria and Cilicia in which Paul and Barnabas had been engaged (1:21) was a sign of God's blessing on this new direction and therefore on the way in which they went about it. The mission to the Gentiles was not to include imposition of the prescriptions of the Mosaic Law.

Those who carefully compare the information presented here by Paul with the narrative account of this meeting given in Acts 15 are puzzled by some of the discrepancies. It does not seem, for instance, that Luke sees Peter's mission as being primarily to the Jews, since in Acts 10 Peter is taught by God in a very direct manner that he need not observe the Jewish rules about clean and unclean foods (Acts 10:9-16; 28-29), and that the Gentile Cornelius and his household have need of his ministry and can receive the grace of God just like any Jewish converts (Acts 10:44-48). Moreover, it becomes known in Jerusalem that he has mingled with Gentiles and he must explain his conduct (Acts 11:1-18). But again Paul may be exaggerating the two sides of the question in order to emphasize that his own mission is definitely to the Gentiles.

"REMEMBER THE POOR."
2:10.

> [10]only they would have us remember the poor, which very thing I was eager to do.

The one proviso laid upon Paul in the agreement according to his own account is that he should be mindful of the poor, and he adds that this is no problem. It is already his desire. This may not be as obvious as it sounds, for the expression does not mean simply to give to those in need. Most scholars agree that "the poor" are the Christians of Judaea for whom Paul organized at least one and possibly two collections of money from most of the Churches of the Diaspora that he had founded (see Rom 15:25-27; 1 Cor 16:1-4; 2 Cor 8,9; Acts 11:28-30 may refer to a prior collection before the writing of Galatians).

There is less agreement on whether the expression "the poor" indicates genuine economic need on the part of those in Jerusalem. Acts 11:28-30 names a famine "over all the world" in the days of the Roman Emperor Claudius (41-57 AD) as the occasion. The universality of the famine may be somewhat of an exaggeration, but however local it was, it must have affected more than just Judaea. There is the added difficulty that, given the slowness of transportation at the time, an undertaking of this magnitude would take months if not years, and would thus not be of much help to alleviate immediate need.

2 Cor 8:14 indicates an equality of exchange: the abundance of the Greek Churches will supply the want of the Jerusalem Church so that the reverse may also be the case. Here again the idea of real need may be present. But Rom 15:27 makes the meaning clear: Jerusalem has shared with the Gentiles its spiritual blessings as place of Jesus' death and resurrection and thus as origin of the Christian movement. As a return gift, the Gentiles can share their material blessings with the Christians of Jerusalem. This is considered a fair exchange, as it is on an individual basis with the material support of ministers (see 1 Cor 9:11,13-14;

Matt 10:10; Lk 10:7; 1 Tim 5:18) and need not imply an actual state of need in Jerusalem. As Antioch was a major missionary center for the Gentile mission, Jerusalem was so for the Jewish mission and it could no doubt make good use of funds in that regard.

Why then are the Jerusalem Christians called "poor" by Paul? Being the representatives of Israel, the inheritors of the covenant, they are symbolically God's poor, the ones for whom Yahweh has a special predilection (Ex 22:23; Is 3:15; 25:4; Ps 35:10; 140:12). The expression thus functions not so much as an economic but rather as a theological title of spiritual privilege, as indeed it often does in the biblical tradition. In other words, it says less about their economic status than about their position of honor among Christians from other communities. However, the impulse of generosity on the part of the Diaspora Christians is also to be underlined.

CONFLICT WITH CEPHAS.
2:11-14.

> [11]But when Cephas came to Antioch I opposed him to his face, because he stood condemned. [12]For before certain men came from James, he ate with the Gentiles; but when they came he drew back and separated himself, fearing the circumcision party.[13]And with him the rest of the Jews acted insincerely, so that even Barnabas was carried away by their insincerity. [14]But when I saw that they were not straightforward about the truth of the gospel, I said to Cephas before them all, "If you, though a Jew, live like a Gentile and not like a Jew, how can you compel the Gentiles to live like Jews?"

In spite of his strong conviction that Christians no longer need observe the Law, Paul has on at least one occasion found himself standing alone on this issue and feeling betrayed by those who had previously backed him up. After the meeting and agreement reached in Jerusalem, even Cephas was apparently convinced that the Jewish food laws need not be observed. The story of Peter and Cornelius in Acts 10 would indicate that he may have reached that conclusion even earlier.

Then Peter went to Antioch, where Gentile presence in the Church was much stronger. There, under pressure from those representing the strict Jewish position in the Jerusalem Church, he withdrew into his former position of observing food laws. By doing this he showed himself to be inconsistent, but because of his prominence he seems to have swayed the entire Jewish membership of the community to do the same, even Barnabas whom Paul had considered his staunchest ally. Paul was understandably irate as he publicly confronted Peter and accused all of them of a lack of integrity. Even though Peter had agreed not to observe the whole Law himself, he was in effect by his actions trying to make Gentiles observe part of the Law by keeping the food regulations.

What is at issue here is not a question of legalism or of inconsequential regulations. The observance of food laws could split a community in two and make it impossible for Jews and Gentiles to sit down together at the same table to share a meal. Because the Eucharist was celebrated in the context of a common meal, it would then be impossible to hold this solemn remembrance together. The very unity and identity of the community as body of Christ were at stake. This is why Paul adamantly and outspokenly opposed anyone who stood in the way of his vision.

III. PAUL'S WAY TO CHRIST: WITHOUT THE LAW 2:15–4:31

JEWS, GENTILES, SIN, AND LAW.
2:15-19.

> [15]We ourselves, who are Jews by birth and not Gentile sinners, [16]yet who know that a man is not justified by works of the law but through faith in Jesus Christ, even we have believed in Christ Jesus, in order to be justified by faith in Christ, and not by works of the law, because by works of the law shall no one be justified. [17]But if, in our endeavor to be justified in Christ, we ourselves were found to be sinners, is Christ then an agent of sin? Certainly not! [18]But if I build up again those things which I tore down, then I prove myself a transgressor. [19]For I through the law died to the law, that I might live to God.

The RSV translation which we are following assumes that Paul's quotation of his words to Cephas ends with vs. 14. This is called into question, however, by the reference in the next verse to "Gentile sinners," an expression probably in current Jewish usage to denote Gentiles in general. It expresses in abbreviated form the selfconsciousness of a people who possess "the sonship, the glory, the covenants, the giving of the law, the worship, and the promises" (Rom 9:4) over against the Gentiles who lack these signs of divine favor (see Matt 26:45). It is the kind of biased expression that goes in an "in-group" but would be offensive to those to whom it refers. Thus it is difficult to imagine that Paul would aim it at a predominantly Gentile readership unless he is being sarcastic, which may indeed be the case. A neat bit of irony would result in vs. 16: it is the sinners (Gentiles who do not keep the Law) who are justified while those who think themselves just (Jews who do keep the Law) are not. One can almost imagine the chuckles that might arise from the Gentile Christians who hear the letter read to them in Galatia.

The other alternative is to take this verse as evidence that large portions of the Galatian communities were Jewish by birth (part of the "we" of vs. 15) but as Christians no longer observed the Law, as Peter himself apparently did (2:14) and Paul as well. In that case the party with whom Paul is in combat is aiming its efforts at Jewish Christians who have fallen away from the Law. This interpretation, however, conflicts with Paul's own statement that his mission is to the uncircumcised (2:7), and his emphasis on the negative effect of accepting circumcision (5:2-3), which would not be an issue for those raised as Jews.

It is very difficult to see where the quote begun in vs. 14 actually ends. The "we" of vs. 15 is still present in vs. 17, but changes to a rhetorical "I" in vs. 18. In any case, the whole passage serves as a transition from narrative of events at Antioch to the theological content of the letter to follow.

Vs. 16 states in one sentence the core of Paul's conviction about the salvation brought by Christ vis-a-vis salvation as promised by the Law. This is the theme that will be developed and exegetically elucidated in chapters 3 and 4 of Galatians and later in the Letter to the Romans (for an even pithier summary, see Rom 3:28). The end of the verse alludes to Ps 143:2 in a way that gives us a first glimpse of Paul's way of using scripture (see Introduction). Here the passage is worked in subtly and indirectly, meant to elicit a response of recognition from the reader who is well versed in the

Hebrew scriptures. The verse in Ps 143, however, says simply that "no one shall be justified before you"—period. There is no mention of the works of the Law. Paul is consciously adapting a general assertion to his own particular interpretation (see also Rom 3:20).

Vs. 17 brings us another example of diatribe style (see comment on 1:10). It is the Law that protects from sin. If because of our faith in Jesus Christ we claim that we do not need the Law, then are we laying ourselves wide open to sin, and even allowing Christ to be one who makes it easier to sin? This possibility is of course unacceptable. Moreover as vs. 18 goes on to say, if what was once rejected as inadequate, i.e. the sense of personal security that comes from obeying the Law, is brought back to center stage and given some importance, then that very return to what was once rejected is an admission that the innovation was wrong. This is why Paul was so upset with Peter's regressive actions at Antioch. His falling back into the old way of observing food laws necessarily implied a sense of guilt about not observing them. Once a step is taken in the direction of responsible freedom, there can be no turning back without an implicit admission that the step taken was a mistake.

Vs. 19 reflects in a synthetic manner a great deal of Pauline theology about the scope and effect of the Law. It is powerless to give life because its whole impact is that of restriction, forbidding, and awareness of sin (see Gal 3:21-22; 2 Cor 3:6; Rom 3:20). So the Law itself leads to a dying process which results in life in God for those who are faithful to it. Even more so for the Christian, who abandons the death-dealing Law in favor of the new life in Christ (see Rom 7:4). It must be emphasized here as elsewhere that Paul's excessively negative attitude toward the Mosaic Law is quite different from that of the faithful Jew who sees it as the means of life in God. Paul seems driven to this de-emphasis on the salvific function of the Law in reaction to his total emphasis on the unique and universal salvific function of Christ.

MEANING OF THE CRUCIFIXION.
2:20-21.

> [20]I have been crucified with Christ; it is no longer I who live, but Christ who lives in me; and the life I now live in the flesh I live by faith in the Son of God, who loved me and gave himself for me. [21]I do not nullify the grace of God; for if justification were through the law, then Christ died to no purpose.

This is the first of several allusions in Galatians to the cross as not only instrument of Christ's death but also as a symbol that is powerfully at work in Paul's life and preaching (see also 3:1; 5:24; 6:12,14). There is some evidence that even outside Christian circles crucifixion was sometimes used as an image of heroism and total self-sacrifice. Even so, Paul's allusions give evidence of a remarkable theological development in the twenty-odd years between the death of Jesus and the writing of Galatians. The most horrible and shameful means of criminal execution has been transformed into a positive image for spiritual growth. It must have been originally as jarring as if I were to speak of my life of prayer as death in the electric chair.

One of the chief characteristics of Paul's spirituality is revealed here. The earliest Christian preaching was of the resurrection and exaltation of Jesus as the Christ. Death was that through which he had to pass in order to enter into that glory. But already Paul is giving equal weight to the death of Jesus as not only important for our salvation but also paradigmatic for the Christian's experience, his own first of all.

Crucifixion means death, and Paul has passed through the kind of death that enables him now to live with a whole new perspective. This dying and coming to a new way of life is begun and dramatically symbolized in baptism (Rom 6:3-4) but lived out in the daily experiences of struggle and surrender.

The almost lyric quality of vs.20, especially of the second part, suggests that Paul may be at least partially quoting

here a brief section of a liturgical hymn. We have seen above
in 2:16 how smoothly he can incorporate into his text a
biblical reference. He could very easily do the same with
a familiar liturgical refrain. Another factor that may indicate a quotation from someone else in the second part of the
verse is the use of the word "flesh" to mean mortal life.
Though Paul does sometimes use the word in this sense
elsewhere, his more frequent flesh-spirit dichotomy (see
3:3; 5:16-21) understands "flesh" as everything in us, whether
physical or psychological, that is opposed to the ways of
God, whereas "spirit" is that in us which is open to God.
Nor is Son of God one of Paul's favorite titles for Christ.
Though he frequently refers to Jesus as son, he uses the
formal title only here and in 2 Cor 1:19 and Rom 1:3 (the
latter is probably a credal formula).

Paul concludes this part of his argument by restating
the case he has been making. He will not cripple the effec-
tiveness of the grace of God by regressing into observance
of the Law. If the Law were able to bring full salvation,
then Christ's death need not have been redemptive. It would
therefore be senseless, and this cannot be. The relentlessness
of Paul's logic here comes full circle.

CHALLENGE TO THE HEARERS.
3:1-5.

> **3** O foolish Galatians! Who has bewitched you, before
> whose eyes Jesus Christ was publicly portrayed as cruci-
> fied? ²Let me ask you only this: Did you receive the Spirit
> by works of the law, or by hearing with faith? ³Are you so
> foolish? Having begun with the Spirit, are you now ending
> with the flesh? ⁴Did you experience so many things in
> vain?—if it really is in vain. ⁵Does he who supplies the
> Spirit to you and works miracles among you do so by
> works of the law, or by hearing with faith?

Paul's anger at the situation in Galatia shows itself once
more in this outburst of frustration. The series of quick
questions is not only typical of the diatribe style, but is

also indicative of Paul's mood: he would like to take his hearers one by one and pin them against a wall until they admit the stupidity of their vacillating conduct.

Commentators have drawn attention to the association of the Greek word for "bewitched" in 3:1 with the folk belief in the "evil eye" as a sinister power. If that is what is meant here, then "before whose eyes" in the following phrase takes on special meaning. The image of Jesus Christ crucified has been openly posted by Paul's preaching like a public notice before their eyes. With this image they were once fascinated, but now someone else has captivated their vision.

The Galatians are asked a question in vs.2 that has an obvious answer. It is meant to embarrass them into admitting the truth. Their reception of the Spirit, probably verified by external manifestations of prophecy, tongues, and other spiritual gifts (vs.5), came as a result of the word that was preached to them by Paul and which they received with faith. Law observance had nothing to do with it. The expression translated "hearing with faith" is a difficult one with many possible meanings: the preaching of faith; the hearing that comes from faith; the hearing which produces faith; faithful listening. Whatever the exact intention of Paul, it is the opposite of what later happened when others convinced them that faith in Christ was not enough.

The Holy Spirit has been given to them as a result of their faith, but they run the risk of returning to "the flesh" (vs.3). Here in contrast to 2:20 Paul is using the word in his favorite sense, as that which wars against the spirit. But he is at the same time creating a play on both words. "Spirit" in vss.2 and 5 is clearly the Spirit of God. In vs.3 it is both the Holy Spirit and the human spirit which is opposed to "the flesh." Similarly, "flesh" is what is opposed to God but it is also sarcastically associated with circumcision, the mutilation of the flesh (see Phil 3:2-3), and thus with the Law.

The following passage from Rosemary Haughton's *Theology of Experience* was brought to my attention by a friend as I was preparing this manuscript. It speaks eloquently of Paul's intention in this passage.

Paul's problem with the Galatians was that they were allowing themselves to be persuaded by Judaizers that their experience of conversion and freedom in Christ was not sufficient; they must also keep the old Law. Paul's answer to this (3:1-5) is an appeal to their own personal experience. On this occasion he doesn't tell them what is the case, though he was not noticeably reluctant to invoke his own authority when necessary. He asks them to judge the matter for themselves, because he has no doubt whatever of the outcome, if they honestly answer his question: "Was it because you practiced the Law that you received the Spirit, or because you believed what was preached to you?" Having asked that question, and knowing what the answer must be, he goes on to support and reinforce the conviction it must bring, by elaborate exegesis and theological argument. But the appeal is first to experience, the rest comes to elucidate what is already known, though perhaps not recognized. And this appeal to experience remains valid for us, even if we non-Jews find the supporting rabbinical arguments niggling and far-fetched.
(*Theology of Experience*, Newman Press, 1972, p. 13)

ABRAHAM, FATHER OF BELIEVERS.
3:6-9.

[6]Thus Abraham "believed God, and it was reckoned to him as righteousness." [7]So you see that it is men of faith who are the sons of Abraham. [8]And the scripture, foreseeing that God would justify the Gentiles by faith, preached the gospel beforehand to Abraham, saying, "In you shall all the nations be blessed." [9]So then, those who are men of faith are blessed with Abraham who had faith.

Here Paul begins his scriptural exposition to prove his point from biblical authority. As Rosemary Haughton has suggested, we may indeed find some of Paul's proof-texting far-fetched. That is because it is based on a method of biblical exegesis which, though time-honored in Jewish tradition, is unfamiliar to most modern Christian readers (for further explanation, see Introduction).

Paul builds his argument for the inefficacy of the Law on a series of biblical quotes and familiar comparisons. The keystone of the structure is Gen 15:6 as quoted in vs.6. Abraham believed the promise of God that his descendants would be numerous even though it seemed humanly impossible. His faith was seen by God as righteousness.

One of our problems in trying to understand Paul's meaning is that English has two words to translate the Greek word used here: righteousness and justification. The first implies a quality that is possessed. The second implies rather something that is bestowed by another.

Perhaps both meanings come together here. Because of his faith in God's seemingly impossible promise, Abraham is father of all those who live by faith, principally of course the Gentiles who rely on faith in Christ rather than the Law. Paul claims that it is the Gentiles who believe in Christ who are referred to in Gen 12:3, quoted in vs. 8. The promise intended by Genesis to refer to Israel has passed over to the Gentiles. What is stated rather succinctly here is developed more fully in Romans 4, which should be read in conjunction with this passage. There it becomes clear that part of Paul's argument is that circumcision was only given to Abraham as a sign of the covenant *after* he had already shown himself to be righteous because of his faith (Gen. 17). Because faith came first and was perfectly adequate, it does not need the Law.

DELIVERANCE FROM THE CURSE.
3:10-14.

> [10] For all who rely on works of the law are under a curse; for it is written, "Cursed be every one who does not abide by all things written in the book of the law, and do them."
> [11] Now it is evident that no man is justified before God by the law; for "He who through faith is righteous shall live";

[12]but the law does not rest on faith, for "He who does them shall live by them." [13]Christ redeemed us from the curse of the law, having become a curse for us—for it is written, "Cursed be every one who hangs on a tree"— [14]that in Christ Jesus the blessing of Abraham might come upon the Gentiles, that we might receive the promise of the Spirit through faith.

The blessing under which Abraham and his faithful followers lie stands in sharp contrast to the curse under which those living according to the Law find themselves. Dt 27:26 is appealed to in vs. 10 with the familiar formula for scriptural quotation. In keeping with his method of exegesis, Paul is able to take the passage out of its context and claim validity for it in a new context of his own making. Thus for Paul the curse extends to all who live by it, in contrast to the blessing to those who live by faith.

Further proof that the Law does not bring justification is offered by the quote from Hab 2:4 in vs.11, and from Lev 18:5 in vs.12. Though Habbakuk intends to oppose life through faith to life in pride and arrogance, Paul transposes the passage to a different situation and opposes faith to life under the Law. Leviticus proposes that keeping the commandments of the Law brings life, but Paul understands the text quite differently, to say that the basis upon which the Law rests is not faith but deeds. Thus a statement which in Leviticus is meant to be positive and freeing becomes, as Paul uses it, quite negative.

Those who come under the curse of the Law are now freed from it by the death of Christ which pays the ransom, for Christ has bought us back from the enslaving power of the Law. Elsewhere too, Paul speaks of the price paid by Christ for our freedom (Gal 4:5; 2 Cor 6:20). It is difficult to tell to what degree he intends this language as a figure of speech. He may be making a comparison to something that would have been quite familiar to his readers: the freeing of slaves through sacral manumission. In this system, a slave who is to be free is fictitiously sold to a god with the deity's temple priests as witnesses and legal transactors. The freed slave has technically been transferred from a human to a divine owner. His freedom is therefore lived out under the patronage and protection of the god. The analogy to Christ who redeems us from the Law is attractive. Whatever Paul's intention, it is surely not to portray God as a cruel and exacting master who requires the suffering and death of his son as appeasement. The emphasis is rather on the loving action of Christ.

Christ has bought us back and freed us from the curse of the Law by himself passing under that curse and taking it upon himself. Again Paul has a biblical passage to illustrate his point. Dt 21:23, quoted in vs. 13, brings down a curse on one who is publicly condemned and hanged as a criminal. Because of the need to avoid defilement in the Jewish community, the corpse of such a criminal must not remain overnight on the tree. Jesus as the crucified one hanging on the tree of the cross thus incurred the curse of the Law. By taking the curse upon himself he was able to rob it of its power. The image of the scapegoat (Lev 16:5-22) may be alluded to here. The sins of the people áre symbolically transferred to the victim and thus removed from the community.

Strictly speaking it is not the Gentiles who need to be redeemed from the curse of the Law. It is rather those Jews who no longer put their trust in it but rather live by faith in Christ. The Gentiles are the direct inheritors of the blessing of Abraham (3:8). In vs. 14 both come together: in Christ Jesus the Gentiles come into possession of Abraham's blessing and Christian Jews (Paul's "we") also receive the same blessing of the Spirit through the one faith in Christ that both sides have in common.

FIRST EXAMPLE: THE VALID WILL.
3:15-18.

> [15]To give a human example, brethren: no one annuls even a man's will or adds to it, once it has been ratified. [16]Now the promises were made to Abraham and to his offspring. It does not say, "And to offsprings," referring

to many; but, referring to one, "And to your offspring,"
which is Christ. [17]This is what I mean: the law, which
came four hundred and thirty years afterward, does not
annul a covenant previously ratified by God, so as to
make the promise void. [18]For if the inheritance is by
the law, it is no longer by promise; but God gave it to
Abraham by a promise.

In the text that follows, Paul uses two examples from
human experience to illustrate what he has just demon-
strated exegetically by deft maneuvering of biblical texts.
The first is that of a person's legal will which, once recognized as valid, is not to be tampered with (vs.15). So it is
with the covenant made with Abraham. Because the covenant was ratified by God, its promises remain (vs.17). This
covenant cannot be changed, added to, or otherwise tampered with by the Law given to Moses several centuries
later.

The exact number of years that Paul establishes between
Abraham and Moses may come ultimately from Ex 12:40,
though that text really speaks of the sojourn of Israel in
Egypt. Biblical tradition on this point is diverse, confusing,
and of no importance for Paul's theological argument.

There is a play on words here that is lost in the English
translation. The Greek word *diathēkē* renders both "will"
in vs.15 and "covenant" in vs.17. One meaning was a legal
contract between two parties, hence, a covenant. Another
was the testimony of a single person, hence, a will. Somewhat a mixture of the two is a third later meaning with which
we are most familiar: testament, that is, official document
of witness. In this regard we speak of the Old and New
Testaments. But the ratified will of vs.15 and the ratified
covenant of vs.17 are really identical expressions with
slightly different meanings.

The whole passage is complicated, however, by the interpretation of Gen 12:7 that is inserted in vs.16. Both in
Hebrew and in Greek the Genesis text uses the collective
singular for the "offspring" (literally, "seed") of Abraham.

Paul takes advantage of this grammatical singular to interpret the text according to his line of argument: the one true descendant of Abraham, the one true inheritor of the promise, is Christ, who as a corporate personality contains and represents all those who faithfully believe in him (Gal 3:29). It is possible that this is not only a clever *tour de force* on Paul's part, but the echo of an already existing rabbinic exegesis of the Messiah to come as embodiment of the promises made to Israel through Abraham. It is also possible that the Genesis text is deliberate in its choice of the singular to emphasize the selectivity of the promise in the patriarchal narrative. Of Abraham's two sons, only Isaac, and not Ishmael, was to transmit the promise. If this is true, then Paul is faithfully representing the intention of the author and carrying it forward to show that the divine selectivity rests ultimately on Christ.

PURPOSE OF THE LAW.
3:19-22.

> [19]Why then the law? It was added because of transgressions, till the offspring should come to whom the promise had been made; and it was ordained by angels through an intermediary. [20]Now an intermediary implies more than one; but God is one.
>
> [21]Is the law then against the promises of God? Certainly not; for if a law had been given which could make alive, then righteousness would indeed be by the law. [22]But the scripture consigned all things to sin, that what was promised to faith in Jesus Christ might be given to those who believe.

Between the two examples comes an interlude which reveals much of Paul's thinking about the purpose of the Law. His tendency to concise but loosely connected reasoning is especially evident here and does not help to make the meaning clear.

The question which naturally follows is evidence: if the promise was made to Abraham and intended for Christ, then who needs the Law? What is it doing here at all? "It was added because of transgressions" (vs. 19). The more obvious meaning of this statement is that the Law helps control or keep down offenses against God. That may be part of Paul's thinking, but comparison with his discussion of the role of the Law in Romans reveals that there is much more to it. Paul's negative valuation of the Law leads him to see it as that which causes awareness of sin, that without which we would not know what sin is (Rom 3:20; 4:15). The Law is certainly not itself sin, but is the occasion for recognizing it (Rom 7:7). Even so, it opens the way for grace (Rom 5:20). The Law was a temporary arrangement made to intervene by way of contrast, so that the need for deliverance from sin would be fully acknowledged.

The role of angels in the giving of the Law to Moses the intermediary is a later embellishment in Jewish tradition, perhaps taking its starting point from Dt 33:2. It is reflected in Stephen's speech in Acts 7:53, Heb 2:2, and contemporary Jewish writers.

Vs. 20 is extraordinarily obscure and has given rise to a host of interpretations. The clearest and most widely accepted is as follows. The role of a mediator is to represent both sides of an issue and bring them together. If there are not two parties, each representing a different position and different interests, then the presence of an intermediary has no meaning. In the giving of the Law, Moses was the mediator between the two parties involved, God and Israel. Both sides had to agree to the terms and to their respective roles in the contract: God to watch over and bless Israel, Israel to keep the precepts of the Law. Moses was responsible to each side for the conduct of the other, and to see that both sides kept their promise.

In the case of the promise made to Abraham and held in trust for Christ, the situation is quite different. The promise was given with no strings attached. It is purely and simply a one-sided gift. God is the only one in this case to take the initiative. The response of the believer is faith, but the believer cannot *do* anything to qualify or earn merit. This is the whole basis of Paul's teaching on justification by faith instead of by works.

The intervention of the Law could then be seen as counterproductive, actually preventing the promise from taking effect. Paul vigorously rejects this possibility (vs.21). The Law is intended to do the same thing as the promise, that is, bring life and salvation. Because of the human situation, this is impossible. The awareness of sin brought by the Law as expressed in the scriptures does not eliminate but rather reinforces sinfulness, since with the Law we know our sinfulness and therefore guilt is increased. Under the Law we are caught in the vicious circle of unreachable ideals and thickening guilt that Paul describes more fully in Rom 7:7-23.

SECOND EXAMPLE: THE BABYSITTER. 3:23-26.

> [23]Now before faith came, we were confined under the law, kept under restraint until faith should be revealed. [24]So that the law was our custodian until Christ came, that we might be justified by faith. [25]But now that faith has come, we are no longer under a custodian; [26]for in Christ Jesus you are all sons of God, through faith.

In this passage Paul again takes a familiar example from everyday experience. Upper class Greek and Roman families assigned a custodian or tutor to care for male children. It was the responsibility of the tutor to get a child up in the morning, take him to school, call for him when classes were over, bring him home, and see that he did his homework and was actually learning well. The tutor was usually a slave of the household, yet he held complete authority *in loco parentis* over the son who might one day be his master. This glorified babysitter was in the strange position of holding a considerable power that was strictly temporary over someone to whom he was really socially inferior.

Paul seizes upon this comparison to illustrate the role of the Mosaic Law. It was our custodian or babysitter, instructing us until the time of maturity came with the appearance of Christ. This is our entrance into spiritual adulthood, when through faith rather than through works of the Law we take our rightful places as mature sons and daughters in the family of God. This delightful metaphor will be continued below at 4:1-7.

BAPTISMAL EQUALITY.
3:27-29.

> [27]For as many of you as were baptized into Christ have put on Christ. [28]There is neither Jew nor Greek, there is neither slave nor free, there is neither male nor female; for you are all one in Christ Jesus. [29]And if you are Christ's, then you are Abraham's offspring, heirs according to promise.

The transition from "we" to "you" that has happened between vss.25 and 26 may mean that Paul is temporarily shifting focus from the Jewish Christian problem to the present reality of his Gentile readers, who do not have to be as concerned as he is with problems of the Law. He will return to the "we" form in 4:3.

This whole passage should be considered in comparison with its two companion pieces, 1 Cor 12:13 and Col 3:11. Our coming to maturity in Christ is both symbolized and actualized by our incorporation in him through baptism. While the passage in Colossians does not refer explicitly to baptism, there is sufficient structural similarity with Gal 3:27-28 and 1 Cor 12:13 to conclude that all three arise out of a baptismal context, and may even be paraphrases of a baptismal formula. All three passages contain an affirmation of Christ as the reconciliation of the opposites into unity.

The language of "putting on" is common to Gal 3:27 and Col 3:9-10. Though such a practice is definitely attested only much later, this expression may already refer to the custom of removing one's clothes before immersion in the baptismal water and putting on a new white garment after ascending from the pool (see Rom 14:13; Eph 4:24).

The three polarities in vs.28—Jew-Greek, slave-free, male-female—reveal to us where the social tensions lay in early Christianity. The first two reoccur in 1 Cor 12:13 and in Col 3:11, in the second case with some elaboration. They are meant to indicate the two extremes of a question in much the same way as Paul does with broader categories in 1 Cor 1:27-28. It is often pointed out that the sequence in which the pairs occur is the same as that in which they are discussed in 1 Cor 7:17-28: circumcision and uncircumcision in vss.17-19; slave and free in vss.20-24; the male-female relationship for the not yet married in vss.25-28. All of this suggests a common underlying formula with which both writer and readers are familiar.

The tension between Jews and Gentiles (functionally the same as "Greeks" here) should by now be evident. This is the major social problem that plagued the first Christian generations, the one to which Paul devoted nearly all his missionary effort and theological reflection. At the time of Paul, Christians in many parts of Palestine and surrounding areas still thought of themselves as a sect within Judaism. But it was already becoming obvious that the future of Christianity lay with the Gentiles who were receiving the message and joining the group in greater numbers than the Jews. This is reflected in statements such as that of Paul in Gal 2:7-10 and Luke's account of the Jerusalem meeting in Acts 15.

Already in Paul's day the success of the Gentile mission was evident and could only be interpreted as the work of God. But it still took several decades before a total break occurred, before Christianity clearly saw itself as a movement apart from Judaism and Judaism totally repudiated its offshoot. Even so, Jewish Christianity, that is, the attempt to interpret the Christ event more in Jewish than in Hellenistic terms, persisted in some form until as late as the fourth century.

Paul's ministry is located historically on the way toward the height of conflict. In spite of the incidents, outbursts, and disillusionments of miscommunication, he can affirm that there is no advantage to either side, and that through the baptismal assertion all can be reconciled into unity in Christ Jesus.

One of the characteristics of early Christian communities is that they were composed of people coming together because of their common faith, without regard to relative social rank. Though there is little evidence in the first century for considerable numbers of highly-placed people, still passages like 1 Cor 1:26 must be taken seriously to mean that there were some noble, well-born people in the congregations. Even aside from the rank of aristocracy, however, it must be kept in mind that the society of the first century Mediterranean world was a highly stratified structure founded on slavery and privilege as two opposite poles. Much of the social stratification depended on birth, but a great deal of it also on wealth. One did not change from level to level on the basis of income and lifestyle as easily as in twentieth century American and European society. Yet it was not unknown that someone who had begun as a slave became such a prosperous freedman that he was able either to buy his way into the ranks of the aristocracy, or to be thus rewarded for his magnificent spending on urban renewal projects. Even if he himself did not make it to the top, his son or grandson surely would.

To be a slave in an urban household was certainly not the worst lot. It could mean a safe, comfortable life, much better off than the free poor in the streets. The possibilities of promotion and freedom were high. Yet the question must have arisen again and again, as we know it did at Corinth, whether there was not an advantage even within the Christian community to being freed. After, masters and slaves were expected to pray together and sit down at the same table together as equals. This could not have been easy for either party. Paul's answer in 1 Cor 7:20-24 is clear, and one gets the impression that he was asked the same questions everywhere (see vs. 17). Neither the slave nor the freedman or freedwoman has any advantage before Christ, so each can remain in peace as he or she is. Paul does not exclude, however, the possibility of gaining freedom where possible. (This is the most widely held interpretation of the end of 1 Cor 7:21, though the ambiguous wording may also mean "profit from your present condition," i.e., remain a slave even if you are offered freedom. To decline freedom, however, was often not possible. It was usually the owner's decision alone that determined the slave's status.) Again the assertion as echoed in the formula of Gal 3:28 is that unity in Christ supersedes any social discontinuity.

The last of the three pairs, that of male and female, is more difficult to interpret for a number of reasons, not the least of which is that it is a living tension within the Church today, while Jew-Greek and slave-free in their historical meaning are dead letters. But there are other difficulties within the text itself to be considered first.

The RSV and most English translations are inexact in their rendering of the conjunctions linking the three pairs in Gal 3:28. While "neither Jew nor Greek . . . neither slave nor free" is correct, "no male *and* female" is the correct linkage between the two elements of the third pair. This may be no grammatical accident. The phrase then recalls Gen 1:27 and a Jewish exegetical tradition which sees the first creation account in chapter 1 of Genesis as an expression of the deep unity of humanity as it comes forth from the creating hand of God, a unity which is lost sight of in the sequential creation of man and woman in the second account of Genesis 2.

If the exclamation "no male and female" as part of the early Christian baptismal formula is meant to refer to the original and essential human unity envisioned in Gen 1:27, then it is of the three pairs the most profound, the one whose consequences drive most deeply into the heart of what it is to live in Christ. Paul's message with all three is that there

is equal access to salvation, to the grace of Christ, and that
there is no advantage or disadvantage to belonging to either
side. It is a proclamation that the differences and destruc-
tive tensions that are felt can be overcome, primarily and
ultimately in the final coming of Christ, but also *now*.

Paul did not advocate the overthrow of slavery. It was
left for later Christians to do that. It was a social system that
he never questioned, but only insisted that it be lived hu-
manely. Paul was too busy trying to get Jews and Gentiles
to sit down together to have been able to tackle the pre-
vailing social structure. He cannot be faulted for having
lived at one moment of history rather than another.

Just as Paul did not advocate the overthrow of slavery,
nor did he question the rightness or wrongness of the particular ways of differentiation between the sexes in the
contemporary social order. That, too, was left for another
generation.

Two things must be remembered when we try to understand the meaning of this powerful passage for today. First,
its horizon goes well beyond Galatians or even Paul; the
saying was already in use for the baptismal ritual, which
attempted to summarize and symbolize the whole meaning
of the Christian life.

Second, tensions expressed in the three pairs are those
experienced *within* the Church, not in regard to outsiders.
There is a deep note of realism here. From the beginning,
everything was not perfect. The formula simply proclaims
the vision. It is precisely those conflicts which strike us
from *within* family, home and community that are the most
difficult. It is these that Paul, echoing the faith of many
other early Christians, proclaims can be overcome in Christ,
and that in him unity is stronger than division.

Vs. 29 joins the immediate remarks to their context. Those
who are one in Christ belong to the promise given to
Abraham, since their unity is in faith. Thus they are heirs
of that promise.

LEGAL CHILDHOOD.
4:1-3.

> **4** I mean that the heir, as long as he is a child, is no better than a slave, though he is the owner of all the estate; ²but he is under guardians and trustees until the date set by the father. ³So with us; when we were children, we were slaves to the elemental spirits of the universe.

At this point Paul returns to the comparison of the child and the guardian which he had begun at 3:23 and from which he had temporarily digressed in 3:27-28. As long as the child of a well-to-do family is not yet of age, he differs little from a slave in the household, in that he does not get his own way, but is subject to the authority of others in every respect—even his father's slaves who are delegated to take care of him. Even though he is the heir and will one day be master of all, he is now subject to everyone until the time recognized by his father and by civil law.

As we already know from the first passage on this subject (3:23-26), we the heirs of Abraham's promise are like the child who has been kept back from possession of the inheritance. In the above passage, however, the guardian holding us in check was the Mosaic Law. Here this part of the analogy has changed somewhat. As children, we have been subjected to the "elemental spirits" of the universe. This problematic expression raises doubts among some as to whether the Judaizers whom Paul opposes are preaching a true form of Judaism or some kind of syncretistic religion with Jewish features.

The Greek word *stoicheia*, meaning originally places in a rank or series, must be considered with Gal 4:8-10 where it also occurs, and understood in the light of another Pauline passage, Col 2:8, 20. The least complicated meaning would be that which it has in Heb 5:12: elementary principles of instruction, that is, of the Law. This interpretation would fit well the discussion of food and calendar regulations in Col 2:16-21. That these elements are principles of the "universe" or "world" (*kosmos*) would then align those under the Law with the rest of humanity in need of salvation, as opposed to those who belong to Christ. This use of "the world" is unwieldy, however, and the interpretation that "principles of the Law" is meant here is not accepted by the RSV translators.

Another possible meaning of "elemental spirits" is the physical cosmic forces of the universe: earth, air, fire, and water, or better, the celestial bodies. If this is true, Gal 4:3, 8-10, and Col 2:8 and 10 are speaking of some form of astrology or belief in cosmic forces as influences on human behavior and worship. This interpretation is based on good evidence from Hellenistic popular religion of Paul's day, and almost necessitates the personification of these bodies as some kind of astral deities. Are they the hostile "principalities and powers" of Col 2:15? Gal 4:8-9 makes sense in this context: when you were still pagans you worshiped as gods things that were not; why do you want to fall into the same trap again? In this case the connection with Judaism seems slim, however.

A third interpretation, a modification of the second, recalls the intermediary role given to angels in the promulgation of the Law in some Jewish theology (see comment on Gal 3:19). It suggests that angelic spirits are seen by some Jewish groups as intermediary agents not only of the Law but also of the functioning of cosmic forces. They then take on an image of power that angels never had originally in Jewish tradition. They are beings to be reckoned with in regard to periodic rites in their honor (Gal 4:10; Col 2:16) which could easily be construed as worship (Col 2:18), with an appearance of esoteric wisdom which is really empty human vanity (Col 2:22-23) that leads nowhere. Understandably would Paul cry that the Galatians, who had once received the Spirit of Christ's freedom, have allowed themselves to be enslaved by "beings that by nature are no gods" (Gal 4:8). This interpretation, which seems to best fit the evidence, suggests that the form of Judaism being preached to the Galatians contains some elements of popular piety which may lead to superstitious practices beyond what the

Law prescribed. Some object to this interpretation that Paul would never refer to angels as "weak and beggarly" (Gal 4:9). But Paul is capable of rhetorical flourish for the sake of contrast in other instances (e.g., 3:10,13). There is no reason to suppose he could not also do so here.

ADOPTION.
4:4-7.

> [4]But when the time had fully come, God sent forth his Son, born of woman, born under the law, [5]to redeem those who were under the law, so that we might receive adoption as sons. [6]And because you are sons, God has sent the Spirit of his Son into our hearts, crying, "Abba! Father!" [7]So through God you are no longer a slave but a son, and if a son then an heir.

When the right moment determined by the father had arrived, the young heir would be formally received into adulthood and into his role as co-owner responsible for the administration of the estate. So it is that God signaled the fullness of time according to his plan by sending his Son to bring us into our rightful place as sons and daughters.

Jesus is "born of woman," that is, according to the human condition. The expression cannot be construed to mean that Paul is speaking of the virginal conception of Jesus, for Job 14:1 uses it of humankind in general and Mt 11:11 of John the Baptist. Rather, it is an assertion of the Son's full entry into the human situation in all its weakness.

He is also "born under the Law," that is, of an observant family. He was raised according to the Law and was subject to it in all things. By doing so, he was able to throw off its yoke for those to come after him (see Gal 3:13). By entering fully under its power, he was able to dispel its power. Continuing the comparison of the minor child, then, we through Christ's action enter into our full inheritance, not as children born of the household but as adopted and thus freely-chosen sons and daughters of God through the promise.

The proof that this is so is the gift of the Spirit, sent into our hearts (see 2 Cor 1:22; 5:5). The primary work that the spirit does in the hearts of Christians according to Paul is to enable them to recognize the familial relationship given by the adoption into God's family. It is the Spirit who gives us power to believe that we are indeed sons and daughters of a loving Father and to respond by crying out to him in the confident call of a child to its father: *"abba"*— daddy! (Compare Rom 8:15-17).

The preservation of the Aramaic form in a Greek-speaking tradition is noteworthy and suggests that it held an important place in religious instruction. This familial form of address that is so distinctive of early Christian piety is undoubtedly rooted in Jesus' own example of familiality with God. The prayer given to the disciples who ask to know how to pray (Mt 6:9-13; Lk 11:2-4) assumes the same bold confidence that is evidenced in Jesus' spiritual teachings (e.g., Mt 5:48; 6:1,6,8,32; 10:20,29). It overflows from his own relationship to God (e.g., Mt 10:32; 11:25-27; Lk 22:42) which will become the cornerstone of John's theology (Jn 1:18, etc.). Such a deeply entrenched conviction can only have come from Jesus himself. The simple title, *abba*, here and in Rom 8 is not a solitary word. The use of it is meant to evoke a whole chain of associations in the readers. The form and style of prayer which they have learned from Paul and experienced in the gift of the Spirit flows from this key word.

A word about sonship: Paul's language here is exclusively male, but he would have intended his remarks to apply equally to both men and women. To fully appreciate the comparison that is being made, however, we must remember that in the patriarchal society of Paul's day a son occupied a place of importance that a daughter simply did not have: as heir, administrator, and future head of the household. It is this idea of right of succession and of coming into one's own possession that is conveyed by the language of sonship which Paul used symbolically for all Christians, both male and female.

SLAVERY TO RITUAL.
4:8-11.

> [8]Formerly, when you did not know God, you were in bondage to beings that by nature are no gods; [9]but now that you have come to know God, or rather to be known by God, how can you turn back again to the weak and beggarly elemental spirits, whose slaves you want to be once more? [10]You observe days, and months, and seasons, and years! [11]I am afraid I have labored over you in vain.

The import of this passage has already been explained in conjunction with 4:3 (see above). Though the interpretation cannot be certain, it seems as if there is more going on here than simply Law observance. There is also the added dimension of some kind of popular, perhaps astrological, ritual in honor of intermediary spirits. This is totally unfitting for those who have received the Spirit of adoption and now belong as children and heirs to the Father.

PAUL'S PAST ASSOCIATIONS WITH
THE GALATIANS.
4:12-16.

> [12]Brethren, I beseech you, become as I am, for I also have become as you are. You did me no wrong; [13]you know it was because of a bodily ailment that I preached the gospel to you at first; [14]and though my condition was a trial to you, you did not scorn or despise me, but received me as an angel of God, as Christ Jesus. [15]What has become of the satisfaction you felt? For I bear you witness that, if possible, you would have plucked out your eyes and given them to me. [16]Have I then become your enemy by telling you the truth?

The flow of the argument is suddenly interrupted by a series of personal remarks which are not easy to understand, largely because we are outsiders to the situation. Paul is speaking to people he knows, people who know his story. He says that he has become as they are, which must mean that he himself has abandoned the way of observing the

Law as means of salvation and has come to live more like a Gentile. That this laying aside of his former way of life was personally very costly, we know from his remarks in Phil 3:4-11: whatever was at one time an advantage has now become disadvantage, what was once gain is now loss.

Because Paul has changed radically for the sake of Christ, he can also expect the Galatians to be faithful to that radical change which has been effected in their lives. This remark in vs. 12 is probably related to a theme Paul takes up elsewhere in the language of "imitation." In 1 Cor 4:14-16 he speaks of the Corinthians as children toward whom he feels like a loving father; they should therefore become imitators of him. Earlier he had praised the Thessalonians for doing just that in their process of conversion and learning to live the Christian life (1 Thess 1:6) and in their acceptance of difficulty and perhaps even persecution as a result, in conformity to the experience of the Judaean communities (1 Thess 2:14). The second letter to the Thessalonians uses the same argument to refute those not willing to work for a living (2 Thess 3:7,9). Though these remarks all come from different situations, the basic meaning is clear: let the same pattern of the Christian life be reproduced in you.

A similar message is coming through here in different words. There is the question of Law observance, as noted above. But there is also more: conformity to the pattern of the crucified Christ whom Paul preaches. He recalls that it was because of some kind of physical suffering (literally, "weakness of the flesh") that he preached the gospel to them in the first place. We would like to have more information: what kind of suffering, sickness, or disease? The remark sounds rather negative, as if to say that the only reason he spent time with them was because he was sick and couldn't go anywhere else!

Though some have taken vs. 15 to mean that Paul's problem was an eye disease (perhaps related to the temporary blindness reported in Acts 9:8-9, 17-18), this is really only one guess among many. The saying about potential eye transplants in vs. 15 sounds more like a colloquialism symbolizing great generosity (compare Ps 17:8; Mt 5:29, and our saying, "I'd give you the shirt off my back"). The illness of vs. 13 may be the same as the "thorn in the flesh" of 2 Cor 12:7, which Paul sees as a gift given to keep him humble. (Speculations about this problem range from epilepsy to fierce temptations of lust.) But we cannot even be sure of this identification. When all the possibilities have been exhausted, we must simply admit that the facts constitute a secret among Paul and his contemporaries which they did not find it necessary to hand down to later generations.

That consideration heightens the impression that whatever the problem was, it was socially embarrassing, at least to the point that Paul's incapacity was humanly hard for him to take. But at the level of his life in Christ, this acceptance of weakness formed part of his own understanding of the mystery of the cross (see Gal 2:20; 2 Cor 12:9-10). The Galatians saw him not at his best but at his worst, and the situation caused some difficulty for them as well as for him. But Paul has nothing to complain about in their treatment of him. On the contrary, they took him in just as they would have an angel or even Christ himself (compare Mt 10:40; Jn 13:20; Heb 13:2).

Paul then asks (vs. 15) with that tone of exasperation that we have already heard from him (Gal 1:8-10; 3:1-5): What in the world has gone wrong? You were doing so well—until this! Their relationship was going fine. He had nothing against them (vs. 12) and they nothing against him, or so he thought. But vs. 16 suggests a glint of hostility on their part that Paul at least fears, even if there may be no grounds for it. It is a well-known experience to be greeted with hostility when one feels that the hard truth must be spoken in love. The alienation that can result is at times very painful. This seems to be what Paul is feeling.

THE OPPONENTS CHARACTERIZED.
4:17-20.

> [17]They make much of you, but for no good purpose; they want to shut you out, that you may make much of them. [18]For a good purpose it is always good to be made much

of, and not only when I am present with you. [19]My little
children, with whom I·am again in travail until Christ be
formed in you! [20] I could wish to be present with you now
and to change my tone, for I am perplexed about you.

"They," no doubt the other missionaries against whom
Paul is waging his battle, have come in to devote themselves
with much ado to the Galatians, who have been partially
won over by the attention and effort lavished on them. In
effect, Paul is accusing his competitors of manipulation.
Their wooing of the Galatian Christians is not for the
Galatians' benefit but rather for their own selfish purpose,
to create a dependence on themselves. When the Galatians'
allegiance switches from Paul to this more recent group
of missionaries, as already seems to be happening, they will
find greater demands placed on them than was the case with
Paul. What is worse, they will find that they will not be
closer to Christ, but really alienated or "shut out" from
him because they have opted for the way of the Law (see
Gal 5:2,4).

After this quick and caustic remark, Paul returns to his
personal style. He reassures them (vs. 18) that there is
nothing wrong with giving or receiving a great deal of
attention as long as the motive is sound. The second part
of the sentence reveals that he has his own case in mind.
Both his own reception by the Galatian communities (4:14)
and his affectionate treatment of them come under the
same description, but with very different ends in view.

Paul is accusing his competitors of dishonesty and self-
aggrandizement. We have no other evidence that this is the
case; they· may have been just as sincere in their position
as Paul. They seem to have leveled the same accusations
against him (see Gal 1:10). This mutual namecalling among
Christians of the first generation need not surprise us. Along
with the dreadful betrayals (Mt 26:69-75 and parallels),
open disagreements (Gal 2:11-15), and even petty quarrels
(Acts 15:39) that seem to have occurred, it shows us the
simple humanity of God's instruments even from the beginning of Christianity. The people of the apostolic age are not

as different from us as they are sometimes portrayed. All of this also demonstrates that unity in Christ does not come easily. It is won only at great price.

In vss. 19-20 Paul's delightfully affectionate way of dealing with his people emerges, as does his genuine worry over their welfare. He has just been scolding them rather severely and now appeals to their sense of loyalty to him. If in 1 Cor 4:15 he speaks of his ministry as fatherhood, here is the expectant mother in labor, trying to bring forth to the world a community in which Christ is fully present as witnessed by their faith and way of life.

The images of ministry as spiritual fatherhood and motherhood flow naturally from Paul's concept of his apostolic authority but are not common in the apostolic generation or in the New Testament at all except in the Johannine writings. Mt 23:9 may even be a conscious objection to the notion of this kind of authority among Christians. But the emphasis in Paul's figure of speech here and in 1 Cor 4:15 is on parental love and concern, not authority.

ABRAHAM'S TWO SONS.
4:21-23.

> [21]Tell me, you who desire to be under law, do you not hear the law? [22]For it is written that Abraham had two sons, one by a slave and one by a free woman. [23]But the son of the slave was born according to the flesh, the son of the free woman through promise.

Having broken his theological train of thought for some pointed personal remarks in 4:12-20, Paul now returns to the systematic exposition of his argument. He begins with the rhetorical question of vs. 21 as a way of returning to the biblical text. If the Galatians are taking seriously this invitation to observe parts of the ritual Law, then they must hear what the Law, that is the biblical text of the Pentateuch, has to say. There can be no partial acceptance of Mosaic customs according to Paul. It is all or nothing (see Gal 5:3).

The story of Abraham, his wife and concubine, and their sons is told in Genesis, chapters 16, 17 and 21. It is the basis for an ingenious allegory which Paul is about to develop. In an allegory, every character in the drama symbolizes some element in the present situation which the author is trying to illuminate through appeal to the story. There is a unique feature to this allegory: while the two wives and two sons have roles to play, Abraham plays himself.

Genesis 16 relates that Abraham and his wife Sarah had children and they were both advanced in age. It was therefore quite difficult for Abraham to believe God's promise that his descendants would be many. Nevertheless, Abraham believed and received God's blessing (Gen. 15:5-6).

At this point, however, Sarah in her desperation tells Abraham to take her slave Hagar as concubine, or wife of secondary importance, in order to have children. This suggestion, acceptable in a nomadic society in which having children is the only way to insure security and property rights, is taken up by Abraham. Hagar soon becomes pregnant, treats Sarah contemptuously, and is mistreated by her mistress as a result. She runs away, but is reassured by God that it is all right to return, since her son Ishmael will have many descendants. At this point it looks as if the son of Hagar the slave is the answer to God's promise to Abraham.

But no! Chapter 17 brings the promise that Sarah too will bear a son, Isaac. It is with this son of Abraham's real wife that God will establish his covenant (Gen 17:19,21). Thus Paul sees Ishmael, the son of the slave Hagar, as the one born "according to the flesh," that is, in the normal way and out of concern for an heir to carry on the human family. Isaac, the son of the free wife Sarah, on the other hand, is the one born through God's promise of an heir to inherit not only material goods but also all of the spiritual blessings promised to Abraham. His birth seemed impossible because of the advanced age of both Abraham and Sarah (Gen 17:17; 18:11-14; 21:5-7) and was thus possible only as a special gift of God.

ALLEGORY OF SARAH AND HAGAR.
4:24-27.

> [24]Now this is an allegory: these women are two cov-
> enants. One is from Mount Śinai, bearing children for
> slavery; she is Hagar. [25]Now Hagar is Mount Sinai in
> Arabia; she corresponds to the present Jerusalem, for she
> is in slavery with her children. [26]But the Jerusalem above
> is free, and she is our mother. [27]For it is written,
>
> "Rejoice, O barren one that dost not
>   bear;
> break forth and shout, thou who art
>   not in travail;
> for the desolate hath more children
> than she who hath a husband."

The two women represent two covenants. This is again in
Greek the *diathēkē*, whose ambiguity we have already seen
in Gal 3:15 and 17. Perhaps "dispensations" or "arrange-
ments" would be a better translation here, unless Paul is
thinking of the new covenant promised by Jeremiah (Jer
31:31) and already understood as applicable to Christ
through the eucharistic act (see 1 Cor 11:25).

Since Paul sees submission to the Law as slavery for a
Christian (Gal 5:1), he can say that Mt. Sinai, where the
Law was given, bears children who are under the domina-
tion of the Law and thus in bondage to it. The difficulty
lies in Paul's facile association of Hagar with Mt. Sinai.
He goes on to say that she also represents the historical
Jerusalem, successor to Sinai, whose children are under
the same slavery to the Law. This present-day Jerusalem
will be compared in vs. 27 with the heavenly Jerusalem. The
introduction of Mt. Sinai is totally unnecessary and breaks
the parallelism Hagar-present Jerusalem, Sarah-heavenly
Jerusalem. Perhaps Sinai is brought in because of its association with the Israelites' wandering in the wilderness, just
as Hagar fled to the wilderness when mistreated by her
mistress, and was found there by God (Gen 16:7). In addi-
tion, both Jewish and Arab legends trace the descent of

the nomadic tribes from Ishmael. An alternate reading of the text suggests that the beginning of vs.25 should say: "For Sinai is a mountain in Arabia," which would at least take some of the emphasis off the Hagar-Mt. Sinai identification. Some scholars have suggested that the association naturally sprang up because the local name for Sinai, still reflected in modern Arabic usage, is a word that very closely resembles the name Hagar. This argument is enhanced by the fact that the name of the other woman, Sarah, never appears in Paul's text, though there is no doubt who is meant.

Whatever Paul's reason for introducing Mt. Sinai into his allegory, he quickly transfers the correlation of Hagar to contemporary Jerusalem, where the authority of the Law is actually centered. By contrast stands the Jerusalem on high, the free city, whose children are the inheritors of the promise. She is therefore mother of those who receive the promise through Christ, including both Jews and Gentiles (see Gen 17:6 where it is promised that Sarah will be a "mother of nations"). The image of the true Jerusalem in heaven had already been developed in Jewish exegesis in Paul's day, so that he is no doubt drawing on a familiar idea. In some of the Jewish apocalyptic literature contemporary with the rise of Christianity, it is thought that the heavenly city will descend at the coming of the Messiah, hence the total appropriateness of Paul's use of the concept (for later Christian use, see Heb 12:22; Rev 3:12 and 21:2).

Vs.27 interjects a quotation from Isaiah (54:1) that refers originally to Jerusalem after the Babylonian Exile, a city apparently without resources, that must rebuild on ruins, not only buildings but also pride, faith, and a sense of identity. Nevertheless, she will prosper because of God's favor. Hence she is called sterile and husbandless, yet at the same time miraculously fruitful. The Isaian passage is applied both to Sarah the barren wife who became miraculously the mother of a great nation, and to the heavenly Jerusalem who bears children not according to the flesh but according to the miraculous promise begun with Abraham and fulfilled in Christ.

CONCLUSION OF THE ALLEGORY.
4:28-31.

> [28]Now we, brethren, like Isaac, are children of promise. [29]But as at that time he who was born according to the flesh persecuted him who was born according to the spirit, so it is now. [30]But what does the scripture say? "Cast out the slave and her son; for the son of the slave shall not inherit with the son of the free woman." [31]So, brethren, we are not children of the slave but of the free woman.

Ishmael was born "according to the flesh," that is, by the ordinary human process and with a concern for producing a descendant for Abraham. The miraculous birth of Isaac in the face of human impossibility renders him the one born "according to the Spirit" (vs.29)—note the shift from "according to the promise," which has been Isaac's description up to vs.28. Paul has now slipped into one of his favorite word games, the spirit/flesh opposition (see comment on Gal 3:3 and below, on 5:16-26). Though "flesh" means primarily the human opposition to God, it also includes observance of the Law because of its reliance on performance of certain actions with emphasis on the physical, especially circumcision. It would have done no good to point out to Paul that Isaac too was circumcised (Gen 21:4) and that his schema did not therefore totally fit the data. To an allegorist only the points that do fit are relevant.

The "persecution" of Isaac by his older brother Ishmael is difficult to substantiate from Genesis alone. Gen 21:9 says simply that Ishmael played or laughed at the occasion of Isaac's weaning celebration, though the intention of the text may be "laughed at" or mocked. The enmity shows up more in later pre-Pauline tradition which traces the hostility between Jews and Arabs to hostility between the two founding brothers—a tradition which still shows little sign of dying. Paul's "so it is now" alludes to his own difficulties getting his Gentile mission and its pastoral theology accepted among not only Jews but especially Jewish Christians

who insist that the Law is the way to Christ. Throughout
the New Testament period, however, the evidence we have
indicates that Christians suffered more problems with
Jewish than with Roman authorities. That tide later turned
in the second and third centuries, and by the fourth century
the Jews found themselves a minority persecuted by a
Christian Roman government.

Paul's punchline comes in vs.30 with his quote of Gen
21:10. Sarah could not tolerate Ishmael's mockery of her
son Isaac and commanded Abraham to cast Hagar and her
son out of the house, which Abraham reluctantly did. The
key question is inheritance. Only the son of the free woman
can inherit Abraham's blessing. Only those whose faith is in
Christ can share in the fullness of that blessing which only
Christ can receive. Paul's theological exposition is complete.

Paul is certainly not the first or only Jew to see extra-
ordinary possibilities of symbolism in the story of Sarah
and Hagar. His contemporary, Philo of Alexandria, a
prominent Jewish philosopher, used the same characters to
work out a quite different allegory. For him Abraham is a
model of one who would advance in contemplative prayer.
Sarah is divine wisdom, by which he cannot be fruitful
until he has first learned human wisdom through the study
of philosophy, which is Hagar. Once he has begotten
Ishmael, the product of the philosophical schools, through
companionship with Hagar, he can then return to Sarah and
profit from her presence by producing Isaac, the true child
of divine wisdom.

Though the purpose and theological framework of the
two allegorists are quite different, there are important points
in common. For both Paul and Philo, Sarah and Hagar
represent two similar but rival categories, and in both
interpretations Hagar and her offspring are clearly inferior to Sarah and hers, as is the case in the narrative itself.
But for both there is also the element of the spiritual, the
divine, and the liberating in all that Sarah signifies.

This brings us face to face with one of the problems that
we must repeatedly encounter in Paul's theology. He is so
wrapped up in his determination that the Law is no longer

necessary since the coming of Christ that the Law comes off very badly. Slavery, death, awareness of sin—these are his associations with the Law that arise out of the perspective he is stressing. They are not all the associations that the Law carries for a believing Jew, then or now. Rather, the Law is God's gift which gives life and points the way to true spiritual freedom. One can then understand why Paul has often been accused through the centuries of totally misunderstanding the true spirit of the Mosaic Law. This remains an unresolved problem for scholars. It would seem that Paul presents the Law in such a bad light because he wishes so strongly to emphasize the total goodness of life in Christ. Compared to this overwhelming gift, nothing can possibly seem worthwhile to him.

IV. THE MEANING OF FREEDOM 5:1-24.

THE YOKE OF THE LAW.
5:1-4.

> 5   For freedom Christ has set us free; stand fast therefore,
> and do not submit again to a yoke of slavery.
>
> ²Now I, Paul, say to you that if you receive circum-
> cision, Christ will be of no advantage to you. ³I testify
> again to every man who receives circumcision that he is
> bound to keep the whole law. ⁴You are severed from
> Christ, you who would be justified by the law; you have
> fallen away from grace.

Now that his theological exposition is complete, Paul
returns to the situation at hand. He does so by opening a
part of his letter that is primarily paraenesis, that is, general
moral instruction, exhortation, and encouragement to lead
a good Christian life. Most of Paul's letters end with similar
sections (see Rom 12:15; 2 Cor 13:5-11; Phil 4:4-9; 1 Thess
4:5, etc.). The keynote here is *freedom*. This is the theme
of the whole of chapter 5, flowing directly from the conclusions reached in 4:21-31. Freedom "is the central theological concept which sums up the Christian's situation
before God as well as in this world. It is the basic concept
underlying Paul's argument throughout the letter" (H. D.
Betz, *Galatians*, p.255). It is, I believe, the keynote and
central theme of Paul's whole theology, the point around

which all else revolves. Because of this fundamental conviction nothing, including the Mosaic Law, can come between Christ and those who believe in him.

Christ has freed us *from* something *for* a purpose. Both aspects of freedom are represented in vs.1. We are freed from any kind of slavery that would cause us to live in fear. Rather, the Spirit that we have received is one of love and confidence (Gal 4:6 and especially Rom 8:15). In keeping with the popular philosophy of his day, Paul did not translate that conviction into a rejection of social slavery, for one's legal and social condition was seen as having nothing to do with one's inner attitude of freedom. Thus Stoic philosophers could suggest that the slave who was not victimized by his own passions could be a far freer person than his master who might be held captive by lust, greed, ambition, and insecurity. Likewise could Paul tell slaves in Corinth that their legal status was no disadvantage but that they should be content with it (1 Cor 7:20-24), and later writers in the Pauline tradition could counsel obedience to a master as a slave's Christian duty (Eph 6:5-8; Col 3:22-25; 1 Tim 6:1-2).

At the same time, our freedom in Christ is goal-oriented. Paul expresses his thought rather succinctly in vs.1 and with seeming repetition. We are freed for freedom, that is, so that our response might be spontaneous, arising from the depths of ourselves. In the concrete situation faced by Paul, for the Galatians to accept any observances of the Law would be regression, a falling back into restrictions and limitations imposed from outside but with serious implications for attitudes and inner life.

There is a solemnity and an insistence in these verses which reveal Paul's absolute determination to prevent all this from happening. The form of vs.1 is the so-called "indicative-imperative" which Paul often uses for his key statements about ethics as the Christian's response to what God has done for us (compare Gal 5:13,25): since this is so, let us respond in kind. Vss. 2 and 3 take on the weight of formal witnessing ("I, Paul. . . testify again"). He is drawing himself up to his full apostolic authority, and this is not the first time on this issue with these people (compare Gal 1:9). Though Paul can be affectionate and even playful at times (for instance, Gal 4:19) he does not hesitate to impose his own authority when he feels it necessary (compare 1 Cor 5:1-5; 6:7-8; 11:6).

In this question of observances of the Law, Paul's emphatic position is that it is all or nothing. Taking on even one of the ritual observances—in this case circumcision—means taking on the whole Law or else it means nothing. And Paul has made it very clear before that the way he sees it, for the Gentile who has never been under the obligation of the Law, acceptance of the Law and freedom in the grace of Christ cannot co-exist. The separation language of vs.4 ("severed," "fallen away") is meant to indicate not rejection by Christ or the community, but rather a decision by which such a person would deliberately alienate himself or herself.

THE WORK OF THE SPIRIT IN FAITH.
5:5-6.

> [5]For through the Spirit, by faith, we wait for the hope of righteousness. [6]For in Christ Jesus neither circumcision is of any avail, but faith working through love.

These verses, like Gal 2:16, are another concise summary of Pauline theology. They are actually a summary of most of what has been said so far to the Galatians. It is through the Spirit that all of the work of Christ is made possible, for it is the Spirit who enables us to see it in action (Gal 4:6) and thus respond. The depth of our response springs from the energy given us by that Spirit, which is faith. This is the effect of the presence of the Spirit in our hearts: that we may believe. Because we are creatures limited by time and space, that is, because we live in history, we cannot experience all at once the new life that has begun in us.

Therefore, though we believe through the gift of the Spirit, we must wait in hope to realize fully what has already been effected.

This already/but-not-yet character of salvation in Paul's theology is developed more fully in passages like Rom 6:3-11. There he speaks of the death with Christ into which we have entered through baptism in order to also share in the resurrection of Christ, though this aspect cannot be fully realized yet. Similarly, Rom 8:18-25 beautifully describes the believers' expectation of that full revelation of what we now hope for in patience. We have already received the first fruits (Rom 8:23), the pledge or guarantee of the Spirit (2 Cor 1:22; 5:5). It is the experience God has already given us that serves as hint or enticement. The best is yet to come.

In the meantime, it makes little difference in what state we are. The first part of vs.6, "neither circumcision nor uncircumcision is of any avail," echoes 1 Cor 7:19 but especially Gal 3:28. The same language is used in its companion passage, Col 3:11. It is the equivalent of "neither Jew nor Gentile," and spans the whole gamut of religious background in Paul's churches. The only thing that is of any use is the response of faith from circumcised and uncircumcised alike.

The priority given to "faith working through love" in vs.6 is not only a moral exhortation to community love. It is also that, as 5:13 and 22 make clear. But it is primarily the recollection that God has first loved us (1 Jn 4:19), that the only thing that enables us to believe in the first place is the love of Christ through the Spirit acting on our behalf (see Gal 2:20; Rom 8:39). We did not begin this, nor shall we end it, but meanwhile our own response is very important.

NEGATIVE INFLUENCE OF THE OPPONENTS. 5:7-12.

> [7]You were running well; who hindered you from obeying the truth? [8]This persuasion is not from him who called you. [9]A little leaven leavens the whole lump. [10]I have confidence in the Lord that you will take no other view

than mine; and he who is troubling you will bear his judgment, whoever he is. [11]But if I, brethren, still preach circumcision, why am I still persecuted? In that case the stumbling block of the cross has been removed. [12]I wish those who unsettle you would mutilate themselves!

The reproach with which Paul begins this section recalls his complaint of Gal 4:15-16: you were doing so well— what went wrong? This time the image of a foot race is used: they got off to a good start but somehow the race has turned into an obstacle course. Again truth is brought into the argument, showing once more that this is not a question of acceptable religious pluralism in Paul's mind, but an issue about which he sees a clear right and wrong. The obvious superiority of his position is brought out by the comparative language: if his side is the truth, the other is a mere "persuasion" (vs.8) which is not from God. The proverb about leaven that he cites in vs.8 also appears in 1 Cor 5:6 with the same connotation of the negative effect of bad company or ideas. It has the same function as Paul's quote from the Greek poet Menander in 1 Cor 15:33, and the "leaven of the Pharisees and of Herod" in Mark 8:15 and synoptic parallels. Paul's assurance that the Galatians will finally come around to his viewpoint (vs.10) may seem strange to us who are accustomed to a more open spirit of dialogue. It is his own form of persuasion. He shows the same attitude elsewhere when it is a question of what he considers an essential point (Phil 3:15 for instance).

He is not always so stubborn. On questions of eating meat that has been offered to idols (1 Cor 8:4-13; 10:14-33) for instance, or the relative value of marriage and singleness (1 Cor 7:6-8, 36-40) he is quite willing to offer suggestions and then let people decide for themselves in their own circumstances. On this question of Jewish customs for Gentile Christians however, as we have already seen at several points, he is unyielding because he sees that the whole nature of the community and the meaning of salvation in Christ are at stake.

Vs. 11 is difficult to understand. Either Paul is proposing a statement contrary to fact as a "what if" consideration, or he did at one time preach the necessity of circumcision. Starting with this sentence and working backwards, we can easily surmise a process of theological development whereby Paul came to his present position regarding circumcision (that is, observance of the Jewish Law) for Gentile converts. It may very well be that he began his Christian preaching with this position not yet clearly worked out, or that he even switched in mid-stream. That Paul is being persecuted, that is, that he periodically gets in trouble with synagogue officials and city magistrates because of his activities, is clear from passages like 2 Cor 11:24-25, 32-33). Part of the trouble may be that he is accused by Jewish Christians of being inconsistent because he has changed his policy—precisely the charge that Paul levels against Peter in Gal 2:11-12!

A comparison of Gal 2:3-5 and Acts 16:1-3 indicates a possible illustration of Paul's previous uncertainty. He maintains in the letter to the Galatians that at Jerusalem he did not yield under pressure and compel Titus to be circumcised. Acts reports that he did just the opposite with Timothy, the uncircumcised son of a Greek father and a Jewish Christian mother, at Lystra in the province of Galatia. If the account in Acts is correct, Paul has recently violated his own principle in the very territory in which he is now defending it. The accusation of inconsistency would then be quite understandable. If Peter heard of it, it would not be difficult to imagine him retorting that Paul should practice what he preaches.

The "stumbling block of the cross" is the scandal of the humiliated and suffering Messiah whom both Jews and Greeks found it impossible to accept because of the contradiction to what they had expected (see 1 Cor 1:22-24). Here the reference is primarily to the Jews (to whom alone the stumbling block is expressly referred in 1 Cor 1:23). The scandal or offense consists in the fact that salvation comes not through the covenant, the Law, and the traditional religion, but through a Messiah who is totally other than all of this, whose earthly appearance bore no resemblance to the power, glory, or wisdom expected to accompany his triumph (see comment above on Gal 2:20 and Introduction). Paul's meaning here is that if he did not take a firm stand against Law observance for Gentiles, then he would be admitting that the Law has some salvific value for them. In that case the death of Jesus would be totally invalidated and would have no power to save.

Vs.12 is a prime piece of Pauline sarcasm: I wish those trouble-makers who place so much importance on cutting (circumcision) would cut a little too far and castrate themselves by mistake! Eunuchs were a known phenomenon in Paul's day, especially in connection with worship of the goddess Cybele and her castrated young lover-god Attis, whose cult had originated in the neighboring region of Phrygia. These eunuch priests of Cybele as well as other eunuchs known from oriental court practice were objects of derision and disgust to Jews and to most Greeks. Paul knows this is a joke that will go over and bring mockery upon his opponents (see Phil 3:2 where he plays a similar trick).

TRUE FREEDOM.
5:13-15.

> [13]For you were called to freedom, brethren; only do not use your freedom as an opportunity for the flesh, but through love be servants of one another. [14]For the whole law is fulfilled in one word, "You shall love your neighbor as yourself." [15]But if you bite and devour one another take heed that you are not consumed by one another.

The key theme of chapter 5 is again recalled. The content of vs.1 is repeated, with both its proclamation of freedom and its warning that freedom can too easily be misunderstood and distorted into slavery that is worse than our previous condition. The slavery of the first part of the chapter is that imposed by the ritual Law, whereas here the threat is of slavery of a worse kind, to the "flesh," whose works are elaborated below in Gal 5:19-21. We have already seen that "the flesh" for Paul is most often that part of our humanity which pulls us away from God (see commentary on Gal 3:2), our fallen nature. This is the case here.

Paul's meaning is that without the detailed precepts of the Law to keep us occupied and tell us right from wrong, we may find ourselves without an adequate structure to give meaning to life and to guide us. Like children without discipline that is imposed from outside, we may regress into the unbridled chaos of selfishness and indulgence. No! Instead, our freedom must find expression in deeds conformed to the Spirit, in self-giving and love, making us figuratively slaves of one another instead of the Law or the flesh.

Paul's radical sense of the identity of Christ and community reveals itself here. We are freed by Christ, and so are more his slaves than anyone else's. Because the community is the Body of Christ, however, that relationship is necessarily lived out in service to one another. The two aspects are inseparable, and find their concrete expression in love (vss.6,13).

Vs.14 is not without its problems. On the face of it, it is simply a quote from Lev 19:18 which fits nicely into the discussion on mutual love, showing that it has a firm biblical base. But having referred to the "whole Law" so negatively in the parallel passage, Gal 5:1-6, how can Paul here turn around and use the same "whole Law" as support for his argument? Perhaps there is a conscious opposition intended: the whole Law is not in the detailed precepts but in the one great commandment of love. Perhaps too, since the Galatians seem to have been willing to accept the idea of a new law to govern their conduct, Paul cleverly guides them in the direction in which he wants them to go by using what appeals to them. He wants to score his point that if they truly love one another, as they are already supposed to do, they do not need the Law because they are already fulfilling the deepest sense of it.

It is important to note that in vs. 14 Paul talks not about doing but about fulfilling the Law, and even then, the verb is passive. It is not our doing but the love-command's being that is emphasized. Love is what it is, and of its very nature it completes and makes perfect the sense, the meaning, the aspirations behind the Law. Paul elaborates on this theme later in Rom 13:8-10 where the same passage from Leviticus is again quoted.

We who know the gospel tradition as a group of written documents know that there Jesus quotes two precepts of the Law as crucial, and the first, love of God (from Dt 6:5), would seem to be even more important (see Mk 12:28-31; Mt 22:36-40; Lk 10:25-28). Why did Paul not do the same? Isn't he leaving out the best half? We have no evidence that he knew the tradition of Jesus' saying about the Law in exactly the same form as Mark received it. He may have only known that Jesus quoted Lev 19:18, the saying about mutual love, and he may be consciously evoking the memory of Jesus' teaching. Even if, as is likely, he did know a tradition of Jesus' sayings about both precepts being the fulfillment of the Law, Paul is probably taking the first for granted as already accepted by the Galatians, whether they accept certain precepts of the ritual Law or not. What he is emphasizing here, in keeping with the tone of paraenetic instruction, is the attitude and responsibilities of persons to one another. Vs. 15 is added by way of colorful contrast; those who live according to the flesh leave themselves open to bestial behavior.

SPIRIT AND FLESH.
5:16-18.

> [16]But I say, walk by the Spirit, and do not gratify the desires of the flesh. [17]For the desires of the flesh are against the Spirit, and the desires of the Spirit are against the flesh; for these are opposed to each other, to prevent you from doing what you would. [18]But if you are led by the Spirit you are not under the law.

At this point Paul begins to be more specific in his description of how grace and human nature work together in a person and a community. The emphatic exhortation to "walk by the Spirit" locates Christianity within the mainstream of philosophical-ethical traditions in the world of Paul's day. Philosophical schools were seen as ways of life in which one proceeded, and the image of walking was a favorite way of expressing the fact that a follower of a certain tradition adopted a distinctive lifestyle that conformed to the tenets of the philosophy.

So popular was the conception of a philosophy as a way of life that the Jewish historian Josephus, a younger contemporary of Paul, could refer to the Pharisees, Sadducees, and Essenes as Jewish philosophies in order to make them understood in the Roman world. Second-century Christian writers frequently did the same for Christianity, knowing that the terminology would have a familiar ring for pagan hearers. New Testament writers use the image of walking for Judaism (Mk 7:5; Acts 21:21—in neither case does the RSV translation preserve the wording) and Christianity (Jn 8:12; 1 Jn 1:6-7; Rom 13:13). Paul uses it in a similar context in Rom 8:4. Remember that the first Christians called themselves followers of the Way (Acts 9:2; 19:9,23; 24:14,22).

Here again as in Gal 3:2-5, the flesh and the Spirit are set in opposition to each other. The companion piece to Gal 5:16-25 is Rom 7:4–8:8. This passage from Romans is extremely difficult to interpret, though most scholars would say that it is a description of what life is like without Christ and the gift of his Spirit. That does not seem to be the case here, where walking according to the Spirit is the ideal proposed from the start. Yet even for the Christian who is in the Spirit because of entry into Christ in baptism, there are problems in the attempt to live according to that Spirit. Spirit and flesh stand in opposition to each other. Remember that for Paul this does not mean Spirit and matter, but rather the two opposing principles or poles within the human personality. For Freud they might have been expressed as Ego and Id, for Jung as Self and Shadow. As has already been said at Gal 3:1-5, Paul uses the word Spirit interchangeably with what seems to us two different meanings: the human spirit as opposite pole to the flesh (for example in vs. 17) and the Spirit of God (as in 3:2,5). Perhaps Paul did not clearly distinguish between the two, while we with more highly developed trinitarian theology and depth psychology find it necessary to do so.

The RSV always capitalizes Spirit in passages on this theme, perhaps wisely since it is usually impossible to be certain exactly what Paul meant. While these comments follow that custom, the ambiguity of Paul's meaning in regard to the word remains. Perhaps too his unclarity on this point is deliberate. If the person in Christ is a new creation (2 Cor 5:17), then he or she is so under the influence of the divine Spirit that it cannot be distinguished whether the impulses toward good come from God or from the person—nor is there any need to know the difference.

That is the ideal, anyway. But even the person living according to the Spirit experiences struggle. Such is the nature of human life in Christ as Paul perceived it. Christ has begun the new creation, but its full blossoming is yet to come. We see only glimpses of it through the experience of the Spirit present and at work in our lives. Because we are led by that Spirit, we do not need the Law as Paul understands it to provide moral guidelines and restrict our conduct. His overriding purpose in the whole letter is to persuade the Galatians not to be deceived into taking on the yoke of the Mosaic Law or any part of it except its command to mutual love (Gal 5:14). That is why even here where the topic is the more fundamental one of how the concrete daily life of the Christian must be lived out, the Law still plays a part as that which is no longer necessary and is therefore to be rejected.

WORKS OF THE FLESH.
5:19-21.

> [19]Now the works of the flesh are plain: immorality, impurity, licentiousness, [20]idolatry, sorcery, enmity, strife, jealousy, anger, selfishness, dissension, party spirit,

²¹envy, drunkenness, carousing, and the like. I warn you, as I warned you before, that those who do such things shall not inherit the kingdom of God.

The next three verses detail what Paul labels "the works of the flesh." They are a good illustration of what has already been claimed with regard to Paul's customary use of the word "flesh." This term is clearly not synonymous with "body" or "matter." Though some of the first and last transgressions in the list involve physical excess, most of the middle terms have much more to do with attitudes and motivation. Such familiar problems as jealousy, anger, and selfishness concern psychological rather than physiological disharmony (compare 1 Cor 3:1-4 where jealousy and strife are the evidence of being of the flesh). "The flesh" is again for Paul that part of us which drags us away from God and the promptings of his Spirit, and keeps us from doing what even our own spirit enlivened by God's grace would prefer to do (vs. 17).

The form of the passage is a familiar one in paraenetic literature. It is often called a "catalog of vices" (or of virtues as in vss. 22-23). Some other examples in the New Testament can be found in: Rom 1:29-31; 1 Cor 5:10-11; 6:9-10; 2 Cor 12:20; 2 Tim 3:2-5; Mk 7:21-22 with shorter parallel in Mt 15:19. This literary form comes predominantly from the Greek philosophical schools but also exhibits the strong influence of Jewish ethical codes when it appears in Christian writings. The presence of idolatry in this list, for example, or of blasphemy in others (such as Mk 7:22, translated "slander" in the RSV) indicates notions that would be more at home in a Jewish setting than a pagan Greek one.

A comparison of similar texts such as those given above will show how often the same vices recur. They are not hand-picked for the occasion. Though there is some variation, the lists can be quite monotonous. This fact gives us one key to the purpose of such collections in early Christian writing. They are conventional pieces brought in wherever helpful to convey a negative impression. They teach moral guidelines only in a general way, for the author can already assume the agreement of his readers that these are indeed undesirable traits and unacceptable conduct. That is why Paul can claim that the works of the flesh are "plain" (vs.19). They are obviously the way his readers do *not* want to be, and in most cases have probably never been.

A second key to the function of such lists in early Christianity may lie in the concluding formula that such people "shall not inherit the kingdom of God" (vs.21—compare 1 Cor 6:9; 15:50). This "kingdom" language, so frequent in the synoptic gospels, is not part of Paul's favorite terminology (other than texts just cited, see only 1 Cor 4:20; 15:24; 1 Thess 2:12; 2 Thess 1:5). It is therefore probable that in such references he is alluding to liturgical or catechetical formulations that both he and his readers know. Some scholars would suggest a baptismal setting in which the new members of the community are exhorted to cast in their lot with the inheritors of the kingdom and not only to avoid such evil conduct themselves, but to refuse to even associate with those who do such things, whether pagan or Christian (see 1 Cor 5:6-13, where the allusions to bread and Passover may also suggest a eucharistic context).

The solemn double warning in vs.21 reinforces the impression that Paul is recalling to his readers something they should already know. The previous warning may refer to a specific occasion, perhaps the time when they were first baptized and instructed. The RSV translation using the simple past, "I warned you before," is grammatically accurate and points in that direction. It is also possible, however, to translate the phrase with the perfect tense, "I have warned you before," which may simply refer to Paul's continual approach and the moral instruction which they have repeatedly heard. In any case, because of the general nature of such a passage, it cannot be assumed that the advocates of Law observance in Galatia are guilty of these moral transgressions.

EFFECTS OF THE SPIRIT.
5:22-24.

> [22]But the fruit of the Spirit is love, joy, peace, patience, kindness, goodness, faithfulness, [23]gentleness, self-control; against such there is no law. [24]And those who belong to Christ Jesus have crucified the flesh with its passions and desires.

Most of what has just been said about the catalog of vices applies in complementary fashion to the catalog of virtues in vss.22-23. If the catalog of vices supplies the overall example of what not to be, the catalog of virtues builds the monument to the ideal Christian, the one in whom the Spirit is allowed free reign. Together these verses explain two opposing alternatives of behavior. Such New Testament passages lay the foundation for a style of Christian moral instruction based on the "two ways" of evil and good, or of darkness and light, which became very popular in early Christianity and influenced such later writings as St. Ignatius' meditation on the Two Standards in his *Spiritual Exercises*. (For more detailed focus on the words used in the two lists, see *Flesh and Spirit* by William Barclay in Suggestions for Further Reading at the end of this volume.)

The desirable traits are rightly called "fruits" of the Spirit, for it is the indwelling presence of the Spirit which produces these delectable results that are meant to be enjoyed. As with the catalog of vices, the actual terms are not carefully chosen but are rather individual pieces of a mosaic which when seen all together carries the total effect.

Each time Paul uses a catalog of vices and/or virtues, he uses it to enhance and illustrate the point he is making. The present passage is no exception. At the end of vs. 23 he returns to his key theme of law and freedom. Law exists to curb evil human tendencies such as those just enumerated, and it is therefore associated with them. Those who are truly freed by Christ for his service need no law to keep them from doing evil, and it is absurd to think of a law to keep us from doing good. When we are completely impelled by the Spirit, there is no law but that of Christ (Gal 6:2). Freely following his law, we know spontaneously the right way to be and do not hesitate to be that way, so that goodness overflows into deeds.

Paul is of course speaking here of the ideal. This is his ethical vision at its most sublime. It is quite clear from other letters that the communities he founded were not perfect, and we need not put them on a pedestal. Some of their members were guilty of unacceptable conduct that was both serious (incest, 1 Cor 5:1-5; gross inconsideration, 1 Cor 11:17-22) and petty (quarreling, Phil 4:2-3). They were no better and no worse than people trying to live together in Christ in any other time or place. But Paul never grew discouraged and never stopped proclaiming his vision of what Christian community can be. It is as valid in our day as it was in his.

After articulating his vision of life in the Spirit, Paul recapitulates by placing the whole picture within the framework of the cross of Christ where he has unashamedly declared himself to be (Gal 2:20). He has come to so identify with the suffering of Christ as a meaningful part of redemption, that he embraces the very means of Christ's death and sees his own life and death as inextricably bound up with the historical crucifixion of Jesus. Here we undoubtedly have spirituality that is unique to Paul. What he has proclaimed much earlier in the letter as his own destiny in the shadow of the cross, he now pronounces to be the situation for all who belong to Christ. (For a more detailed study of crucifixion and its symbolic use in the ancient world, see *Crucifixion* by M. Hengel, listed in Suggestions for Further Reading at the end of this volume.)

That powerful element in human nature which opposes and resists the power of God has been put to death by entrance into baptism, which is participation in the death of Christ (Rom 6:3,6). Once that death has been undergone, the only possible direction is forward into the new life of the Spirit (Rom 6:4,5). There can be no turning back, either into unworthy conduct in relationships—which is really more of an issue at Corinth than it is here—or into dependence on ritual as part of the way to God—which has been very much the issue in Galatia. The passions and desires of the flesh are just as much for the security of knowing one is doing the right thing as they are for gratification of the sensual appetites.

V. GENERAL INSTRUCTION
5:25 – 6:10

MUTUAL SUPPORT.
5:25–6:2.

> [25]If we live by the Spirit, let us also walk by the Spirit. [26]Let us have no self-conceit, no provoking of one another, no envy of one another.
> **6** Brethren, if a man is overtaken in any trespass, you who are spiritual should restore him in a spirit of gentleness. Look to yourself, lest you too be tempted. [2]Bear one another's burdens, and so fulfil the law of Christ.

When taken in the context of what has gone before, vs.25 is one of the strongest and most penetrating statements in the whole letter. Like 5:1 and 13, it is in the form of the "indicative-imperative" (see comment on 5:1). The verse is both a summing up of all of chapter 5 and an introduction to 5:26–6:10. It echoes 5:16 and completes its thought. The RSV renders "walk by the Spirit" in both 5:16 and 25, and it is correct in assuming that the meaning is similar. The Greek words, however, are different. While Gal 5:16 uses the more familiar term for proceeding along a chosen path (see comment on 5:16), the word used here literally means to "draw up in line" and may be meant to convey a military image of soldiers assembled in rank, or simply the idea of diverse elements acting together. Paul uses it in the same way in Gal 6:16; Rom 4:12; Phil 3:16.

The meaning of Gal 5:25 is clear even though not easy to follow. It is a plea for consistency between what we believe and how we live, what we say and what we do. It goes still deeper: Paul is not only telling his readers to practice what they preach. He is also declaring that God is greater than all of us. The work of the Spirit has already changed us into who we are in Christ, whether we are always aware of it or not. We live by the Spirit not only to the extent that we consciously allude to the fact, but also by the presence of the Spirit in our very being through baptism, in our person and our community, and through us in the world.

Some very practical conclusions follow regarding Christians' treatment of one another. The ethical maxims of Gal 5:26–6:10 are bits of common wisdom that with a few changes would be at home among Jewish sages or Greek philosophers. Yet the whole passage bears the stamp of Paul's own wisdom and experience, and his desire to see his beloved people living according to their commitment. This section, like Gal 5:19-24, has nothing apparently to do with the commotion in Galatia over the Law and the teachers and missionaries to whom Paul so violently objects. The only times that we are brought back to that situation are the points at which Paul ingeniously inserts comments about law: 5:23 and 6:2.

Gal 6:1 seems to refer to procedure for some kind of community correction. There are other instances in the New Testament of a slowly forming tradition to meet this need which would surely have arisen (Mt 18:15-18; Jas 5:16,19) but this is probably the earliest. In communities with loose organization and no definite lines of authority, what could be done with individuals who violated commonly-accepted norms? While a great deal of diversity along these lines may have been tolerated at first, some limits had to be set, and in fact the early history of Christianity shows an ever increasing tendency toward the enforcing of conformity within local groups and eventually throughout wide regions among churches that were in communion with one another.

Paul's description of his readers as "spiritual" may be a bit of irony since he has repeatedly reproached them for giving in to the flesh (Gal 3:3; 5:13,16; see the interesting contrast in 1 Cor 3:1). On the other hand, he has also declared that they are in the Spirit (5:25) and that they have received the signs of the Spirit's presence and power (3:2, 5; 4:6). While the title "spiritual" may sometimes refer to those who have the gift of prophecy (as perhaps in 1 Cor 14:37), it is usually said of the whole community, as is the case here.

Gal 6:2 has become axiomatic in Christian tradition as indeed it deserves to be. The idea of sharing one's burdens with others is not original with Paul, but it certainly expresses succinctly the concrete and practical aspect of what the Body of Christ means. It is a two-way ideal, and can only contribute to the bond of community if this is kept in mind. Generosity prompts most of us to be eagerly willing to help carry the burdens of others to the extent possible. Allowing others to share our burdens is somewhat more difficult for our independent spirits. Yet both aspects are contained in Paul's exhortation. Both elements are part of the law of Christ.

The appeal to this law of Christ is somewhat puzzling after all of the vigorous assertion about freedom from law in which Paul has been engaged. It may be simply a clever way of rounding out his argument by using the same terms, as he does in 5:23. In Rom 3:27 and 8:2 he seems to do the same thing, with the "law of faith" (translated "principle" in the RSV) and the "law of the Spirit" respectively (compare Jas 1:25). Similarly, in 1 Cor 9:21 he defends himself against the charge of lawlessness by describing himself as not totally without law since he has rejected the Mosaic Law, but rather "under the law of Christ." Other early Christian traditions stressed the law of Christ as alternative to the Jewish Law, for example Matthew's deliberate portrayal of Jesus in the Sermon on the Mount as giver of new precepts to replace the old ones (Mt 5:21-22; 27-28; 31-36; 38-45).

It is also possible that in his use of the idea of the law of Christ, Paul is borrowing an expression of those teachers with whom he disagrees. Though they advocated observance of at least part of the ritual Law of Moses, they seem to have considered themselves no less adherents of Christ, and therefore were just as attentive to his teaching. They may very well have taught a combination of obedience to the Mosaic Law and the Law of Christ. In any case, Paul's meaning is that Christ's law is one of love, not rituals, and the only way to fulfill it, that is, express its true meaning, is to behave lovingly towards one another.

PERSONAL INTEGRITY.
6:3-5.

> [3]For if any one thinks he is something, when he is nothing, he deceives himself. [4]But let each one test his own work, and then his reason to boast will be in himself alone and not in his neighbor. [5]For each man will have to bear his own load.

The three maxims in these verses all represent traditional practical wisdom and can stand independently of one another. The first, an appeal to self-knowledge (vs.3), is a favorite theme in Greek philosophical teaching, as is the warning that serious deception lies in thinking one is somebody. The popular maxims of the philosopher as well as those of the biblical Wisdom tradition show keen awareness of the fragility of human life and the stupidity of vain pretensions. Paul refers more frequently to this theme particularly in 1 Corinthians where the tendency to self-deception seems to have been more pronounced among some of the troublemakers (1 Cor 3:18; 8:2; 10:12; application to himself in 2 Cor 12:11).

The second maxim (vs.4) exhorts the reader, again in the terms of conventional wisdom, to mind his or her own business. Self-examination will show both the mercy of God and the misery of human existence, but whatever is to be boasted about must be something for which personal responsibility is taken. Boasting is a favorite theme for Paul, but he always insists that the reason for boasting is not our own achievements but God's accomplishments in us (for example, Rom 3:27; 15:17; 1 Cor 5:6; Phil 1:26; 2:16; and especially 2 Cor 12:1-10).

The third maxim (vs.5) seems at first sight to contradict the ideal of mutual support held up in 6:2, and indeed there is a difficult weaving of independence and interdependence in vss.1-6. But actually the present verse comes out of an entirely different line of thought and uses different terminology. The meaning here is not that we cannot help others or allow them to help us, but that ultimately all of us are responsible for our own gifts and talents, problems and suffering. We are all accountable to God for the decisions we make and the attitudes we hold. This responsibility no one can take from us.

TEACHER AND COMMUNITY.
6:6.

>⁶Let him who is taught the word share all good things with him who teaches.

Vs.6 is put forth in the singular for the sake of literary style, as the previous five verses have been. It is nevertheless meant as a general maxim applicable to community situations as well as individual relationships. The sharing of material goods was an important ideal in some of the Hellenistic philosophical schools, as it was in the early Church (Acts 2:44; 4:32). Moreover the principle that the ministry of the gospel deserves material support in return is strongly upheld in early Christianity upon the authority of Jesus himself (1 Cor 9:14; Mt 10:11 with its parallel, Lk 10:7; 1 Tim 5:18).

The function of the teacher in apostolic communities was an important one, placed only after that of apostles and prophets by Paul (1 Cor 12:28). The itinerant apostle evangelized and kept up communication between churches. The prophet was the impromptu voice of the Spirit in the midst of the community, confirming, supporting, and challenging according to the inspiration given to him or her. The teacher was responsible for regular and ongoing instruction in the day to day living of the Christian faith, for interpretation of the Scriptures and formation to liturgical leadership. Teachers were immensely important persons, called to their role because of their learning, judgment, and wisdom. They are the catechists of primitive Christianity. On them rested the burden of continued transmission of knowledge and formation to faith after the missionaries had moved on—as is still the case in areas where the Church is not widely established. In exchange for their gift of spiritual ministry, they are entitled to a share of material necessities from those they serve.

DIVINE COMPENSATION.
6:7-8.

> [7]Do not be deceived; God is not mocked, for whatever a man sows, that he will also reap. [8]For he who sows to his own flesh will from the flesh reap corruption; but he who sows to the Spirit will from the Spirit reap eternal life.

Another maxim follows, interpreted through Paul's own spirit-flesh juxtaposition. God's justice and ultimate power are invoked to remind the reader that in the end nothing will escape the divine all-seeing eye. The final result of a human life will grow organically out of everything that has gone before. The agricultural language of planting and harvesting may have been closer to the experience of ancient readers than of modern ones. The point nevertheless comes through quite clearly: what we have been in life is what we will be at death. This does not of course exclude the phenomenon of deathbed conversion, but does relegate it to the realm of the unusual.

The neat metaphor Paul intends in vs.8 is better seen if the translation runs, "he who sows *into* his own flesh" . . .

"but he who sows *into* the Spirit." The agricultural image is that of placing the seed *into* the ground and then harvesting *from* the same ground. Modern readers could transpose the comparison to the world of the stock market and probably understand it even better: the one who invests in "the flesh"—that is, selfish enjoyment, pride, etc.—will be paid in dividends from the same source, whereas the one who invests in "the Spirit"—in love, joy, and gift of self—will receive its dividends of eternal life. Succinctly stated, you get what you pay for.

EXHORTATION TO GOOD DEEDS.
6:9-10.

> [9] And let us not grow weary in well-doing, for in due season we shall reap, if we do not lose heart. [10] So then, as we have opportunity, let us do good to all men, and especially to those who are of the household of faith.

Continuing the farming metaphor, Paul encourages his readers to perseverance and courage. When the time comes for reaping, that is, at the return of Christ, the present labor of sowing and cultivating the seed will pay off. Vs. 9 is essentially an eschatological admonishment, as are vss. 7-8. It is in the final reckoning, which Paul believes will come in his lifetime, that the fruit will be harvested. This passage enlarges on and completes the more obscure thought of vss. 4-5. At the end, each one stands responsible for what he or she has done with the seed.

This kind of thinking is common in eschatological exhortations. It is the answer to the question, what to do til the end comes. In a radically apocalyptic perspective, time becomes something to be endured. Paul is not so negative; for him, what we do in the in-between period also has immense value. Hence the admonition of vs. 10: while we are waiting, let us take every opportunity to do good, remaining always of course within the perspective of Christian freedom and of the relativity of human efforts in the light of all that

Christ has done for us. This is no doing that loses sight of God's initiative and submerges itself in the accumulation of good deeds. Rather, the good which we are to do is merely the best response we can make to him who loved us and died for us while we were clearly not worth it (Gal 2:20; Rom 5:6-11).

The exhortation to do good to all is seemingly restricted in the next breath to concentration on Christians. Paul does not mean to negate the open attitude of benevolence to all which is a characteristic mark of most of early Christianity. Rather, this last comment focuses the effort within a realizable framework. "Charity begins at home," as the proverb goes. Those closest and most familiar to us can be the most difficult to love, but they are the point of departure for our love's expression.

VI. CONCLUSION AND RECAPITULATION. 6:11-18.

PAUL'S SIGNATURE.
6:11.

> [11]See with what large letters I am writing to you with my own hand.

Up to this point Paul has been dictating to a secretary who has done the actual writing for him. This was not an uncommon practice for him (compare Rom 16:22; 1 Cor 16:21; Col 4:18; 2 Thess 3:17). He may have dictated word for word as one does in the case of something so important that every word counts. For some letters, on the other hand, he may have turned over an outline of what he wanted to say to someone he trusted to accurately convey his thought, as one does with a competent and creative secretary. That is how some would explain the differences in terminology and style in some of the Pauline letters such as Colossians and Ephesians. Because Galatians is filled with personal references and a style of address that is quite blunt in tone, it is more likely that it was directly dictated by Paul himself.

The "large letters" with which Paul writes are somewhat of a puzzle. Some commentators suggest that he cannot write in a careful script because his hands are more used to craft work and are not skilled in penmanship. Others would see the expression as a means of emphasis: because what he has to say here is vitally important, it will be written in larger handwriting. In either case, Paul seems to be writing the conclusion of the letter himself, and this is quite understandable, for the final eight verses are an admirable summary of the key points Paul has been trying to make in all that went before.

SUMMARY OF THE LETTER.
6:12-15.

> [12]It is those who want to make a good showing in the flesh that would compel you to be circumcised, and only in order that they may not be persecuted for the cross of Christ. [13]For even those who receive circumcision do not themselves keep the law, but they desire to have you circumcised that they may glory in your flesh. [14]But far be it from me to glory except in the cross of our Lord Jesus Christ, by which the world has been crucified to me, and I to the world. [15]For neither circumcision counts for anything, nor uncircumcision, but a new creation.

The theme of the letter has been Paul's defense of his way of preaching the Gospel against others who insist that some observances of the Mosaic Law must be imposed on Gentile Christians. Here Paul attacks the motives of these other teachers by accusing them of simply wanting to make a good impression "in the flesh," that is, according to human standards rather than those of God. With reliance on circumcision and the ritual Law as part of the means of salvation, Paul's opponents do not have to rely totally on the free grace of Christ. Even more, they do not have to see in the mystery of Christ's suffering and death on the cross the only real way. Paul is convinced that the two ways, the Law and the cross of Christ, are incompatible. They cannot be combined.

Since his opponents placed emphasis on the necessity of circumcision and thus acceptance of the Law, they came off looking very good to the Jewish authorities and to the staunch Jewish Christians who were apparently the majority in the mother church of Jerusalem. These are the people with whom Paul had to contend during his visit there (Gal 2:3-5) in spite of the recognition given to Paul's mission and theology by the leaders in that community (Gal 2:6-10). Paul's insistence on freedom from the Law and total reliance on the redemptive death of Christ brought him trouble wherever the Jewish Christian position was strong. He was thus always vulnerable to hassling from this powerful element in the Church, while his opponents were not.

The word "persecution" is usually associated with trouble from the Roman government. That is not the case here. It is rather a question of persecution from Jewish authorities and Jewish Christians at a time when Christianity's distinctiveness from Judaism was not yet clear.

The meaning of vs.13 is uncertain. Those who accept circumcision but do not keep the Law may be those Gentile Christians who have been swayed by Paul's opponents and now want to make converts of the rest. More likely the description refers to the opponents themselves who are not orthodox Jews but live a kind of in-between existence in which they accept part of the Law but not the whole of it. This position would include Peter (see Gal 2:14), though it is not therefore to be assumed, as has sometimes been done, that Peter is the ringleader of the Jewish Christian position to which Paul is opposed (contrast the concessionary attitude of Peter in Gal 2:9).

Certainly Paul's opponents do themselves practice circumcision, even if they do not adhere to all the prescriptions of the Law. Otherwise their advocacy of circumcision would carry no credibility. But Paul is again accusing them of insincere motives. Not only do they hold their position to avoid trouble (vs.12), but all they really care about is victory. They want to be able to glory (actually, to boast—see comment on Gal 6:4) in their own success in persuading others to adopt their position.

Paul has accused his opponents of selfish manipulation (4:17), cowardice (6:12), and now of being on a power trip (6:13). His judgments in this regard need not be taken at surface value. He is clearly biased against them and may not even know them personally. Attributing unworthy motives to one's opponents is a characteristic of much ancient theological debate and particularly of the kind of rhetoric in which Paul is engaged. It is unfortunate that none of the argumentation directly from the other side has survived. We really have no reason to doubt that these teachers were as sincere and as zealous as Paul even though their theology was very different.

By contrast to Paul's portrayal of his opponents, he asserts that there is only one focus for *his* boasting: the cross of Christ, that is, what God has done for us through the redemptive suffering and death of his Son (recall again the comments and references given at Gal 6:4). In previous references to the cross of Christ in Galatians, Paul has seen it as symbol of salvation (3:1), as that which gives meaning to the Christian's existence (2:20), as means of dealing a fatal blow to the forces for evil within us (5:24), and as sign of contradiction (6:12). In vs.14 he adds a new creative use of the image, a further step from its use in 5:24. While the other references lead to identification of the believer with Christ, 5:24 and 6:14 treat the cross as what it most basically is, a means of putting to death. If in 5:24 it is the flesh which is killed on the cross, here it is the world.

Through the agony of the cross, the world is as good as dead as far as Paul is concerned, and he is as good as dead in regard to the world. The antipathy of the world to the cause of Christ is a theme more strongly developed in John's Gospel (for instance, Jn 8:23; 12:31; 14:17; 15:18; 17:9). But the idea does appear elsewhere in Paul (see Rom 3:6; 1 Cor 1:20,21; 2:12; 3:19). In these passages as here in Gal 6:14, the "world" is everything in human experience which is futile and hostile to our real destiny.

In this whole passage Paul jumps rapidly from one idea to another. Vs.15 reverts back to the thoughts of vss.12-13 and again succinctly summarizes the whole argument of the letter. The new creation is the new beginning for humanity that is brought about by Christ (compare the use of the same expression in 2 Cor 5:17). It is Christ who has undone the damage done by the first man, Adam. Christ the new Adam makes all things new—a clean start, as if the human race were coming fresh again from the hand of the Creator. Thus anything to do with the former arrangement, such as the Mosaic Law, has no significance.

There is a parallel statement in 1 Cor 7:19 which ends quite differently. There it is not the new creation that matters, but keeping the commandments of God, presumably the Ten Commandments, the moral Law. The passage in Galatians is the more radical, but the two are not contradictory. With his declarations about freedom Paul never meant to imply abandonment of the moral Law which for the Jew is inseparable from the ritual Law. But Paul had a very different way of approaching ethics, not through precepts but through giving oneself over entirely to the power of the Spirit. He firmly believed and experienced that the person who lived totally in the Spirit of Christ would spontaneously know and do the good without a law to dictate it. When writing to the Corinthians Paul is concerned not with explaining his stance against the Mosaic Law but with formation to Christian ethical sensitivity. In Galatians the issue is the theological one of the role or non-role of the Law. Hence the difference.

BLESSING AND WARNING.
6:16-17.

> [16]Peace and mercy be upon all who walk by this rule, upon the Israel of God.
>
> [17]Henceforth let no man trouble me; for I bear on my body the marks of Jesus.

Vs.16 is the first of two concluding blessings (there is another in vs.18). This particular blessing formulation is unique in the Pauline writings and has stimulated much discussion among scholars, especially because it bears a remarkable resemblance to one of the blessings of the Jewish petition prayers in the ancient synagogue liturgy, the Shemoneh Esreh. The Jewish liturgical prayer runs: "Give peace, happiness, and blessing, grace and mercy and compassion to us and to all Israel your people." Though it is uncertain how old the synagogue prayer is, variations of the same form were undoubtedly in use in Paul's day, and he seems to be either quoting one or allowing its influence to spontaneously form his own prayer. If this is so, the irony of the situation should not be overlooked. While arguing for the ineffectiveness and anachronism of the Jewish Law, he uses a Jewish liturgical blessing formula in a letter to Gentiles. This apparent discrepancy is part of the complex pattern of extensive Jewish scriptural, theological, and liturgical influence on the early Christians even as they gradually but inevitably moved away from their Jewish roots.

The "rule" by which the recipients of the blessing walk is perhaps better understood as a standard or criterion against which to measure one's belief and way of life. The standard is the cross of Christ as symbol of a new era and a totally new way of relationship with God.

Who is the Israel of God? This is a strange expression from the pen of Paul, one that occurs nowhere else in his writings. It can hardly mean the Jews. Although later in Romans 9-11 he will take up the question of their fate, that is not a topic discussed in Galatians, and the Jews would have been the last to abide by the standard of vss.14-15. Paul must then refer to Christians of some kind, whether Jewish or Gentile. Though he never uses this expression elsewhere, he does speak of the Jews as Israel "according to the flesh" (1 Cor 10:18), and this phrase should probably by inference

be contrasted to Phil 3:3: "For we are the (true) circumcision, who worship God in spirit. . ."(the word "true" is the
RSV's interpretation, not found in the Greek). Rom 9:6
makes it clear that Paul is selective in his understanding
of who really belongs to Israel: only those who can receive
the promise through faith. These are his "Israel of God,"
and they are for the most part Christians.

Though he never comes right out and says it, Paul implies
in several unconnected statements that Christianity is the
true Israel. It is still too early in Paul's day for such an idea
to catch on. The relationship with Judaism is still evolving.
A century later Christian writers will begin to quite consciously see themselves as the replacement of Israel, the
true inheritors of the covenant. This is a development that
is full of ambiguous consequences. It opened the way for
the institutionalization of Christian worship in imitation
of the Temple sacrifice and priesthood of the Old Law. It
stimulated Christian hatred of Jews by portraying them
as those rejected by God because of their hardened hearts.
While Paul would not have intended either result, some of
his ideas laid the groundwork for both.

We can only attempt to conjecture how much Paul realized what he was saying with his language of the new creation and the (real) circumcision. We would like to know
to what extent he was conscious of beginning something
entirely new, a new religion. His thoughts are small seeds
which would bear fruit in later years.

Vs. 17 is the flip side of the preceding verse. Blessing and
curse often go together in biblical language. The blessing
of vs. 16 gives way to an implied curse on those who think
differently from Paul and try to hinder him from preaching
his message. The marks (*stigmata*) of Jesus which Paul bears
on his body have been variously interpreted. The remark
probably alludes to tattoo marks borne in the Greek and
Roman world sometimes by slaves branded by their masters, particularly runaway slaves. The slaves of a temple

might also be branded with the mark of the god or goddess, and sometimes a deity's devotees would voluntarily brand themselves as a practice of private devotion. Soldiers also occasionally branded themselves with the name of their commander for the same reason.

Paul says that he bears the marks of Jesus on his body. Some have understood this to refer to an early Christian practice of tattooing a cross on one's body as a sign of dedication. It is difficult to see, however, how Paul could have gone along with such a practice, given his abhorrence of circumcision and contemptuous rejection of the Law's rituals as belonging to the flesh. It is more likely that Paul is referring here to the physical effects of his labors and the suffering he has had to endure in his missionary work (see 2 Cor 4:8-12), or even more specifically to the effects of several beatings (2 Cor 11:23-25). These are physical scars which manifest the dying of Jesus (2 Cor 4:10).

The aspect of ownership marks should not be lost sight of, however, for it is probably the basis of the image. Slaves who are branded are marked as someone's property and anyone who tampers with them is violating property rights. The warning with which vs. 17 begins says exactly this: Paul is marked by his scars as the property of Jesus Christ. Anyone who interferes with him will have to answer to his owner, Christ himself.

The idea that these marks of Paul are the mystical gift of the wounds of Christ, as the stigmata came later to mean technically, dates only from the biographers of St. Francis of Assisi and should not be read into Paul's text.

CONCLUDING PRAYER.
6:18.

> [18]The grace of our Lord Jesus Christ be with your spirit, brethren. Amen

As in all his letters, Paul ends with a formal blessing, a wish for the spiritual prosperity of the readers, people for whom he feels real affection in spite of the disturbing events that have happened. The abruptness of the conclusion, however, and the absence of personal remarks and greetings (contrast 1 Cor 16:5-24; Rom 16: Phil 4:21-23) still indicates his irritation and uneasiness of communication with them.

The final Amen, though fully attested in the oldest manuscripts of the text, may have been added later as a congregational response when Paul's letters were read out loud during community worship. It is a concluding affirmation of the message of love, freedom, and participation in the life and death of Jesus Christ that Paul wishes to convey in his letter to the Galatians.

SUGGESTIONS FOR FURTHER READING

Detailed, Scholarly Works

Betz, Hans Dieter, *Galatians*. Hermeneia Commentaries; Philadelphia: Fortress Press, 1979. An excellent all-new scholarly commentary nevertheless quite comprehensible to the serious non-expert. The best of its kind in English.

Earlier important articles on Galatians by the same author:

"2 Cor 6:14–7:1: An Anti-Pauline Fragment?" *Journal of Biblical Literature* 92 (1973) 88-108. Argues that this passage really represents the position of Paul's Galatian adversaries.

"Spirit, Freedom, and Law: Paul's Message to the Galatian Churches," *Svensk Exegetisk Arsbok* 39 (1974) 145-60.

"The Literary Composition and Function of Paul's Letter to the Galatians," *New Testament Studies* 21 (1975) 353-79.

"In Defense of the Spirit: Paul's Letter to the Galatians as a Document of Early Christian Apologetics," in *Aspects of Religious Propaganda in Judaism and Early Christianity* (ed. Elisabeth Schüssler Fiorenza; Notre Dame: University of Notre Dame Press, 1976) 99-114.

Burton, Ernest De Witt, *A Critical and Exegetical Commentary on the Epistle to the Galatians*. International Critical Commentary; New York: Charles Scribner's Sons, 1928, vol. 35. An older but good scholarly commentary based on the Greek text.

Lightfoot, Joseph Barber, *Saint Paul's Epistle to the Galatians.* London: MacMillan and Co., 1st ed. 1865; reprint of 10th ed., 1892. An old but still helpful commentary on the Greek text by a renowned British scholar of the last century.

Commentaries Intended for More General Reading

Ahern, Barnabas M., C.P., *The Epistles to the Galatians and to the Romans.* New Testament Reading Guide; Collegeville, Minnesota: Liturgical Press, 1960, vol. 7. One of a standard pamphlet series with brief but rich commentary.

Bligh, John, S.J., *Galatians, A Discussion of St. Paul's Epistle.* Householder Commentaries; London: St. Paul Publications, 1969, no. 1. Thorough, lengthy in-depth, but non-technical.

De Wolf, L. Harold, *Galatians: A Letter for Today.* Grand Rapids, Michigan: Wm. B. Eerdmans, 1971. A sensitive portrayal of Galatians in the light of contemporary American social problems. Paperback, 86 pages.

Guthrie, Donald, *Galatians.* Century Bible, New Series; London: Nelson, 1969. Detailed verse-by-verse commentary on the RSV text, with extensive introduction.

Neil, William, *The Letter of Paul to the Galatians.* Cambridge Bible Commentary; Cambridge: University Press, 1967. A short and very readable commentary based on the text of the New English Bible.

Quesnell, Quentin, *The Gospel of Christian Freedom.* New York: Herder and Herder, 1969. A short exploration of Paul's teaching on freedom by means of the text of Galatians.

Ridderbos, Herman N., *The Epistle of Paul to the Churches of Galatia*. New International Commentary on the New Testament; Grand Rapids, Michigan: Wm. B. Eerdmans, 1956. An extensive and detailed but clear commentary.

Special Topics

Barclay, William, *Flesh and Spirit: An Examination of Galatians 5:19-23*. Nashville, Tennessee: Abingdon Press and London: SCM Press, 1962. Explanations of the words used in Paul's catalogs of vices and virtues, by one of today's most popular New Testament commentators.

Hengel, Martin, *Crucifixion in the Ancient World and the Folly of the Message of the Cross*. Philadelphia: Fortress Press and London: SCM Press, 1977. A brief and informative study of the facts and symbolism of crucifixion in the Greco-Roman world.

Stendahl, Krister, *Paul Among Jews and Gentiles*. Philadelphia: Fortress Press, 1976. A very helpful collection of essays that attempt to ground Paul's theology of Christ and justification in his own experience rather than in the way later Christian theologians interpreted him.